THE TWELVE MOST IMPORTANT WORDS

Jeff Frick

THE TWELVE MOST IMPORTANT WORDS

A Transformative Guide That Will Benefit All Relationships

Jeff Frick

The Twelve Most Important Words by Jeff Frick
Copyright © 2025 by Jeff Frick
All Rights Reserved.
ISBN: 978-1-59755-841-9

Published by: ADVANTAGE BOOKS™
                      Orlando, FL, www.advbookstore.com

All rights reserved. No portion of this book may be reproduced, stored in a retrieval system, or transmitted in any form or by any means—electronic, photocopy, recording, scanning, or other—except for brief quotations in critical reviews or articles, without the prior written permission of the publisher.

All Scripture quotations, unless otherwise indicated, are taken from The Holy Bible, New International Version, NIV. Copyright 1973, 1978, 1984, 2011 by Biblica, Inc. Used by permission of Zondervan. All rights reserved worldwide. www.Zondervan.com. The "NIV" and "New International Version" are trademarks registered in the United States Patent and Trademark Office by Biblica, Inc.

Library of Congress Catalog Number: 2025939801

Name:	Frick, Jeff., Author
Title:	*The Twelve Most Important Words*
	Jeff Frick
	Advantage Books, 2025
Identifiers:	ISBN Paperback: 978159758419
	eBook: 9781597558617
Subjects: Books ›	Religion: Christian Life - Inspirational
	Books › Religion: Church Leadership
	Books › Religion: Adult Education

GRAM Ministry
48366 Whatley Court
Shelby Township, MI 48315
248.431.4051
Gramministry@gmail.com / Gramministry.org

First Printing: July 2025
25 26 27 28 29 30   10 9 8 7 6 5 4 3 2 1

Table of Contents

PRAISE FOR THE 12 MOST IMPORTANT WORDS 7
DEDICATION 11
FOREWORD 12
ACKNOWLEDGEMENTS 13
AUTHOR'S NOTE 15

1: UNAWARE OR UNWILLING? THE UNSPOKEN WORDS HURT THE MOST 19
- -Why are you here- 22
- -Standing or running- 25
- -When lies become truth- 27
- -My way or the highway- 30
- -It's your fault- 32
- -Complete loss of control- 35

2: I WAS WRONG 39
- -Only God- 40
- -It almost didn't happen- 44
- -Not willing to wait any longer- 46
- -God is still with you- 48
- -Scratching old scars- 51
- -Something must change- 53

3: I AM SORRY 57
- -First funeral- 61
- -Operator error- 63
- -On someone else's behalf- 65
- -Never have I said- 69
- -One and done- 72
- -A promise made- 74

4: PLEASE FORGIVE ME 79

- -Houston in Italy- 80
- -Horrible husband- 82
- -Talking invites healing- 85
- -The impossible choice- 88
- -Saying goodbye- 90
- -Relationship restored- 92

5: I LOVE YOU 95

- -Stolen backpack- 97
- -Not your yes man- 100
- -Wanting but not receiving- 102
- -Homeiromai- 105
- -Sons and daughters- 108
- -The hidden blessings of God- 110

6: WALLS ELIMINATED? 115

- -When the real work begins- 117
- -The 3 responses to walls- 119
- -Psalm 139- 123
- -Not for one minute- 127
- -iOS18- 130
- -No regrets- 131

SALVATION PRAYER 135

SCRIPTURE REFERENCES 137

OTHER BOOKS BY JEFF 141

ABOUT THE AUTHOR 143

Praise for The Twelve Most Important Words

"'The 12 Most Important Words' is a transformative guide that will benefit all relationships in your life. Jeff illuminates the power of humility, accountability, and love through twelve simple yet profound words, that if practiced have the power to change your life and the life of those around you. These twelve words have sadly fallen out of use in our world today, and I believe a resurgence will ignite a more tangible and undeniable witness of Jesus Christ. I know you will be blessed by this book. And if not – I was wrong – I am sorry – Please forgive me – I love you!"

Rev. Dr. Brian Mowrey, Sr. Pastor - Kensington Church

****

"I have known Jeff Frick for several years and consider him a close friend and brother in Christ. Together we have served, hugged, laughed, cried, prayed, taught, and fought. Simply put, he is a straight shooter who tells the truth. Everything in this book is true and reflects Jeff's willingness to answer God's call and go into the arena. The Jeff Frick I read about from the past compared to the one I know today is a testament to the transformative power of God's Grace in Christ, and Jeff responding, 'Send Me Lord.' As I was reading 'The 12 Most Important Words,' I couldn't help but to think that everyone needs to know this, and to live this way. I have engaged in fellowship with hundreds of men over the last 15 years. In my observation, there is an epidemic of relational damage that has occurred because people have not lived by 'The 12 Most Important Words,' and because of that, hurt people…hurt other people. It is sad to think of someone unequipped or unwilling to say these life-giving words, in a sincere way, and back it up with lasting change. 'The 12 Most Important Words' is not only a training manual for breaking down relationship walls, it is full of incredible stories that will awaken your heart and draw you closer to God and your true self."

Dave Halsey, Co-Founder & President - The Band of Brothers Michigan

"In 'The 12 Most Important Words,' Jeff Frick delivers a deeply personal and scripturally rich exploration of humility and forgiveness. This book is a must-read for anyone longing to rebuild broken connections and strengthen their walk with God. It's a timely reminder of God's design for reconciliation."

Erik Bledsoe, Founder & President - Take the Hill Ministries

****

"In His response to a certain lawyer's question about inheriting eternal life, Jesus emphasized that the most important law is to, '...*love the Lord your God with all your heart and with all your soul and with all your strength and with all your mind; and, Love your neighbor as yourself*' (Luke 10:27 NIV). In this book, 'The 12 Most Important Words,' Jeff helps his readers with relevant scripture, his own insights and personal experiences with how best to go about truly loving your neighbor, your friend and family member. Some of these people are easy to love, but many come with hurts, resentments, deep wounds, animosity, bitterness, and unforgiveness. Listen as Jeff prays, listens, counsels, loves and meets people where they are at and lays a simple, effective framework for restoration, healing, forgiveness and the breaking down of barrier walls. Many times, Jeff writes from challenging, relational experiences in his own family and with a friend. We have sent many *hurting* brothers his way and plan to put his book in the hands of friends wrestling with painful relationship issues."

Ron and Judy Daggett, Pastor/Mentor/Friends

****

"'The 12 Most Important Words' personally hit home for me as Jeff writes about his son Michael. Vulnerability equals real. Real equals impact. Impact equals change. Jeff's vulnerability isn't just for storytelling's sake. Thus, as Jeff shares his lessons learned, a reader struggling with all kinds of issues can easily apply these easy to understand, but difficult to execute, principles in these 12 words."

Scott Haima, Conference Director - Detroit-Buffalo (ISI) Iron Sharpens Iron/Executive Director - (NCMM) National Coalition of Ministries to Men

The Twelve Most Important Words

"Jeff Frick is a rare and treasured friend, a brother in Christ whose wisdom and dedication to serving the Lord has profoundly impacted my life. For over 15 years, Jeff has poured his heart into pastoral care ministry, leading GRAM Ministry – God Refines All Men, God Redeems All Men, God Restores All Men – with a vision to see men transformed by the grace of God. His previous works, 'How do I Love my *Neighbor*? 4 PROMISES AND 6 TRUTHS' and 'IDENTITY MATTERS- The Power of Belonging,' have already explored the vital importance of spiritual community and authentic connection. This new book, 'The 12 Most Important Words,' promises to be another powerful contribution to those seeking a deeper understanding of God's transformative love.

Jeff's passion for investing in others is evident in every aspect of his life. He encourages men to fully embrace the grace of our Heavenly Father, discover their true purpose, and find their strength in Jesus Christ. He is a gifted leader, adept at creating supportive environments for both individual and group settings, fostering growth and healing.

Jeff is, without a doubt, one of the most dedicated servants of God I know. He lives a life of genuine service, freely sharing his time, talents, and testimony with those in need. He embodies the wisdom of a seasoned contemplative, yet his approach remains grounded in practical, Christ-centered principles. He has been a constant source of mentorship and encouragement in my own journey of faith, offering guidance and counsel as I've navigated various areas of ministry and service. Jeff's humility shines through in all he does, and he readily shares the wisdom he has received from Christ.

The Spirit of the Lord rests upon Jeff and his ministry. Even a brief conversation with him reveals the depth of his commitment and the transformative power of a life fully surrendered to God. 'The 12 Most Important Words' reflects this same spirit, offering powerful insights into themes of self-reflection, communication, forgiveness, and authentic love. Within these pages, Jeff masterfully explores concepts like self-awareness, the impact of our words, the necessity of humility, the hope of redemption, the challenge of apology, the power of forgiveness, the essence of true love, and the potential for reconciliation. He doesn't just present these ideas; he unpacks them from a Christian perspective, offering practical applications that will resonate with readers long after they finish the book.

Jeff Frick

I highly recommend reading 'The 12 Most Important Words.' It is a timely and relevant message for anyone seeking to live a life of greater purpose, deeper connection, and authentic faith. Prepare to be challenged, inspired, and ultimately, transformed by the wisdom contained within these pages."

Todd Gordon, Executive Director - WAVE PROJECT/Elder - Kensington Church

Dedication

This book is dedicated to my two granddaughters who will be born later this year.

Dear Margot Joann and Ava Grace,

Your grandmother and I cannot wait for your arrival into this world. We waited so long for daughters and now our daughters, your mothers, are giving us granddaughters, the both of you. Our hearts are so full because God has blessed us beyond our wildest dreams. The love that you will receive rises above comparison. You will be lights to our family, and in this world, that cannot be snuffed out. We are excited to watch you grow, and to be a part of your lives!

The love of a grandparent may be the closest kind of love that helps us understand the love of God. However, your parents will shower you both as well with nothing but agape love. In fact, there is nothing both of your parents wouldn't do for you, they love you so much!

Your grandmother and I can't wait to spoil you both. We love you dearly!

Blessings,

Grandpa

> *Numbers 6:24-26 (NIV), "The Lord bless you and keep you; the Lord make his face shine on you and be gracious to you; the Lord turn his face toward you and give you peace."*

Jeff Frick

Foreword

I often catch myself in my contemplative moments, dreaming of a world released from the burden of self-protection.

It is certainly not the sublime perfection we will experience in the fullness of our Savior's presence; but perhaps the "front stoop" of our eternal home. It is a world where we still make mistakes, and the pain of those mistakes is still keenly felt. But we somehow have the discernment to recognize our part in causing that pain and the strength of character to admit it and take the steps to make amends.

But where to start?

My friend may have the beginnings of an answer.

I have known Jeff over half of my career in pastoral ministry and count him as a friend and reliable co-conspirator in creating safe, inclusive, and distraction-free environments where people can heal from life's pain and equip for life's adventure.

The convictions he shares in the pages that follow are borne from a life touched by great pain and greater healing. Jeff is a self-admitted "work in progress" whose calling is one of simple availability to others, sharing freely from what he has learned as a fellow sojourner on a path of healing.

The crux of what he shares is universal: Our relationships – and the world – are better when we are honest about our mistakes, vulnerably ask for forgiveness, and commit to loving more completely.

I invite you to shuffle off the burden of self-protection. Master the 12 most important words. Use them with yourself and in your relationships – and take a step into a world I still dream of and the life our Creator intended.

Chris Cook, Director of Care Initiatives - Kensington Church

Acknowledgements

I have many people to thank for helping me in the writing of this book.

I was inspired by God's revelation to write books. He has given me five titles to books He wants me to write. It's pretty amazing that I have now written three books and have never had a personal interest, thought, or goal to write one. God is so incredible!

Many have helped with the most difficult process of editing this book and I would like to thank them. This list is small but mighty, and each of them deserves my gratitude and thankfulness for the countless hours in reading and re-reading this book. The names listed below made it possible for you, the reader, to receive the best achievable product.

Thank you, Chris Bokmuller!

Thank you, Judy Daggett!

Thank you, Ron Daggett!

Thank you, Maria DeKimpe!

Thank you, Dave Green!

Thank you, Tiffany Jameson!

Thank you, Barry Nannini!

Thank you, Steve Perucca!

Thank you, Allison Renaud!

And thank you, Tim Renaud!

Because of all of you, this book is clear and legible to anyone who decides to read it.

> 1 Thessalonians 1:2 (NIV), "We always thank God for all of you and continually mention you in our prayers."

(Sketch by Steve Perucca)

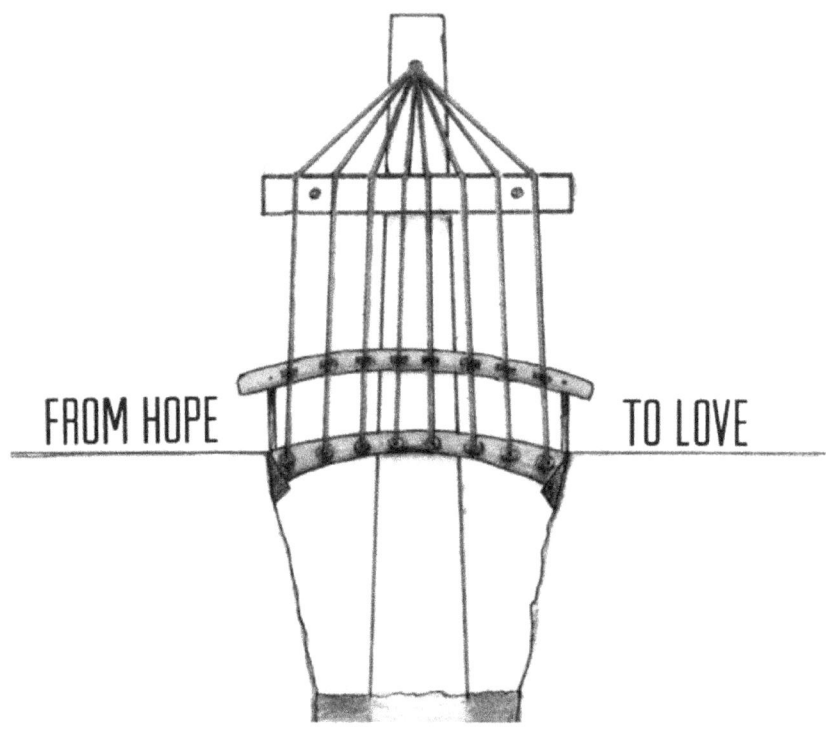

The cross of Jesus is seen as a bridge to reconciliation, offering forgiveness and hope to those who long to close the gap that separates them from their loved ones.

Author's Note

As I was writing this book, I encountered literally dozens of people who were perplexed by their broken relationships. If I tried to capture all the heart-breaking stories I have heard, there would not be enough ink or paper or even a binding strong enough to support such a book. Because our relationships require *constant* work to nurture and protect, I suspect we will always have some broken relationships among us. However, it doesn't have to be that way. We can all learn from our past mistakes and become something that is greater than what we ever thought possible. When we learn to become more, our relationships can also become stronger, more fortified, and more deeply appreciated.

Have you ever considered what is the most difficult instrument that anyone can ever attempt to play? The most difficult instrument that anyone can ever attempt to play is the second fiddle. "Why is the second fiddle the most difficult instrument that anyone can ever attempt to play," you ask? The second fiddle is the most difficult instrument that anyone can ever attempt to play because it requires humility and selflessness. The second fiddle requires us to place others above ourselves. When everyone else is more important than you, we come to find that the world looks vastly different. That's exactly why the 12 most important words are so helpful. "I was wrong, I am sorry, please forgive me, I love you" are words that place more value on the other person than we place on ourselves. When we speak these words often and with great sincerity, our broken relationships can begin to mend, and our healthy relationships will be reinforced.

Indisputably, there are two questions that I hear most often when people come to me to help them understand how to repair their broken relationships. The first question is, "How do I fix this?" The second question is, "How long will this take?" Both questions have no end point and therefore cause us to anguish and maybe even give up before we begin. These questions place the focus on "self" instead of the other person, whom we have somehow harmed. The answers to the questions provide the basis that we use to determine if we will even begin to take the journey of reconciliation. Focusing on "self" is how we got into this mess in the first place because self-preservation *always* places the relationship at a far distant second. However, if we were part of the problem, we should be willing to be part of the solution, no matter how long and difficult the journey may be. We should learn to ask a different question, a much better question, "What *wouldn't* we do to close the gap between us?" This question focuses our attention on the other person. It says that we value the relationship and other person more than we value ourselves. This question articulates that "we" are greater than "me." But instead, most often, we are more concerned with how much it will *cost* us to walk the journey of attempting to mend our relationship. That's where the 12 most important words, "I was wrong, I am sorry, please forgive me, I love you" can help us start the process of reconciliation.

Perhaps you are questioning if the best days of your life are behind you because of the broken relationships in your life? The answer to that question is sometimes determined by the wisdom we gain through time. If we spend our time yearning over the past and make no effort to change the future, we may find that our best days are in fact behind us. But, if we walk with God, no matter our age, our best days are always yet to come. He asks us to model our life after His Son, Jesus. Jesus humbled himself and placed *everyone* else above Him by walking in obedience and laying down His own life for the benefit of *all*.

> *1 John 3:16 (NIV), "This is how we know what love is: Jesus Christ laid down his life for us, and we ought to lay down our lives for our brothers and sisters."*

When we learn to lay down our lives for others the way Jesus did for us, we may find that the 12 most important words, "I was wrong, I am sorry, please forgive me, I love you" are no longer necessary. We may also begin to see generational curses fall away and realize that the relationships we forge today are greater than anything else we could ever leave behind.

> *Philippians 4:4-9 (NIV), "Rejoice in the Lord always. I will say it again: Rejoice! Let your gentleness be evident to all. The Lord is near. Do not be anxious about anything, but in every situation, by prayer and petition, with thanksgiving, present your requests to God. And the peace of God, which transcends all understanding, will guard your hearts and your minds in Christ Jesus. Finally, brothers and sisters, whatever is true, whatever is noble, whatever is right, whatever is pure, whatever is lovely, whatever is admirable—if anything is excellent or praiseworthy—think about such things. Whatever you have learned or received or heard from me, or seen in me—put it into practice. And the God of peace will be with you."*

The Twelve Most Important Words

(Sketch by Steve Perucca)

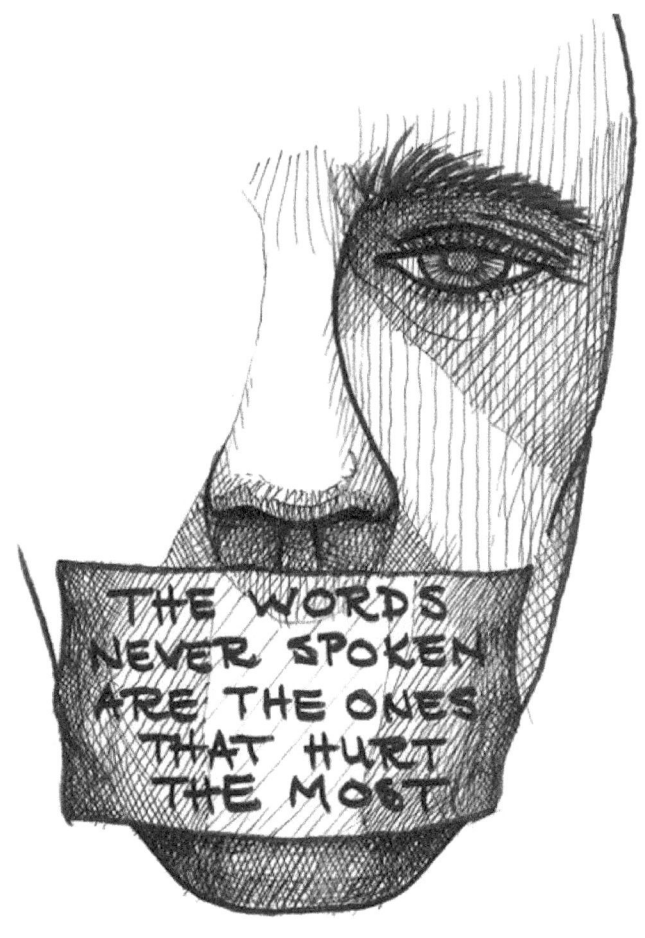

Proverbs 18:21 (NIV)
"The tongue has the power of life and death, and those who love it will eat it's fruit."

1

Unaware or Unwilling?
The unspoken words hurt the most

"It is the highest form of self-respect to admit our errors and mistakes and make amends for them. To make a mistake is only an error in judgment, but to adhere to it when it is discovered shows infirmity of character."
-Dale Turner

Everyone makes mistakes, no one is immune. The world will quickly assess whether you are a wise person or a fool by how you address the mistakes and shortcomings of others. Even more so, how you handle yourself when your own mistakes are brought to light. Are you wise or foolish? Do you feel ashamed and maybe even angry when your shortcomings are uncovered? Being corrected is not easy and doesn't always bring out the best in us. Taking correction and constructive criticism in stride and using it for our ultimate good can only happen if we are regularly practicing being corrected.

Take writing this book for example, I sought out multiple people who could be a resource to me during the "correcting" phase of the writing process. It's not exactly the easiest thing or the most fun thing to have others read something I've poured countless prayerful hours and months into writing that is now being edited through the lens of others with different ideas on how best to phrase my thoughts and vulnerable personal experiences. It's a lot of work to put something together only to have others "tear" it apart in the name of the editing process. Now, this is the third book God has inspired me to write, which means this is the third editing process, better yet, "correcting" process, I've been through. Going through the corrections that have been suggested to me by the multiple people who have agreed to help me through this part of the book writing phase, has been easier this time than it was the first time. I took things more personally the first time and had a harder time accepting the corrections that were being suggested. It was a new endeavor and something I needed to get used to if I were going to be able to fulfill God's calling of writing the five books he laid out for me. With each book, the corrections were easier to handle and did enhance the readability of my books. I know I will be able to say the same of this book after it has gone through the same correcting process the first two went through. I think the same could be said for the "editing" of our shortcomings.

So how do you handle yourself when your own mistakes are brought to light? I think it may be safe to say that our first instinct may even be to cover up our mistakes and spin a story that lessens our error and/or our involvement and in turn, our hope is that it lessens the eventual impact it may have. Again, unless we are *regularly* practicing correction, our typical inclination is to paint a story that makes us look like the *good person* with the best intentions and everyone else as the bad person with lesser intentions. Ignoring our mistakes rather than dealing with them or even placing blame elsewhere to save face are common methods of deflecting the embarrassment we may feel by having our mistakes put on display. We all have good intentions, but most of us lack follow through. That's why our good intentions can still be littered with mistakes and shortcomings that cycle us through all of the same feelings no matter how good our intentions may have been.

> *Proverbs 28:13 (NIV), "Whoever conceals their sins does not prosper, but the one who confesses and renounces them finds mercy."*

Humbly admitting you were wrong, making restitution for your wrongdoing, seeking forgiveness for your failure, and reassuring the injured party that you value them, are the best steps to dealing with correction like a wise person. It's as easy as stating 12 simple words. In fact, I consider them **the 12 *most important* words**, "I was wrong, I am sorry, please forgive me, I love you." Our mistakes can cause us to lose focus of what's truly important, being together **"with"** our loved ones. God knows you will fail in life, but He doesn't want you to be stuck in your failure. So, take action and don't let the hurt of unspoken words engulf your existence or your relationships.

> *Proverbs 24:16 (NIV), "for though the righteous fall seven times, they rise again, but the wicked stumble when calamity strikes."*

Communication and conflict resolution are two of the most critical components of every relationship. Collectively, our culture struggles in these areas, largely because each of us

The Twelve Most Important Words

has a severe, personal addiction to control and comfort to varying degrees. However, we all have the ability to rise up with humility and move on in grace. Unfortunately, far too many of us fail to look at our relationships with our friends, our family, and our loved ones and see them as blessings. We tend to be too worried about protecting ourselves from humiliation instead of loving others. How many millions have never heard the 12 most important words? How many people have been crushed by the weight and rejection of unspoken words? How many relationships have been destroyed because the unspoken words hurt the most?

Perhaps the 12 most important words were never offered to you and that's why you haven't offered them to anyone else? Blaming others for our own delinquency does nothing to help solve the problem. When we are talking about those who *do not* share the 12 most important words, there are only two groups of people; those who *don't* know and those who know but simply refuse to share. If you truly don't know, you only get to use that excuse once. Now that you are reading this book, your excuse is gone. The next time you don't share the 12 most important words with your loved ones, it is no longer an excuse, it's now a choice. If you *do* know the 12 most important words but are waiting for those words to be shared with you before you share them with anyone else, the world will see you, and know you, as foolish. Wanting others to do something for you that you are unwilling to do for them is two faced. Knowledge is gaining understanding; wisdom is learning to apply it.

> *Ecclesiastes 1:18 (NIV), "For with much wisdom comes much sorrow; the more knowledge, the more grief."*

The power to redeem and restore our relationships lies in taking action and speaking the 12 most important words. We all have this power at the tips of our tongues. We all have the same opportunity to mend and repair what has been broken. So why are we so reluctant to wield this power? Don't our loved ones deserve to be treated with kindness, respect, and dignity? If so, let me ask you, "Are you unaware? Or are you unwilling?"

It may be quite possible that some of us have approached our relationships completely wrong from the start. St. Francis of Assisi is believed to have shared this thought, "Preach the Gospel at all times. Use words if necessary." He believed that our actions should be so clear and so profound that our words wouldn't be necessary. Let us learn to use our words "in the *quick*" when our actions have failed us. "I was wrong, I am sorry, please forgive me, I love you," are the words our relationships are totally dependent upon for survival.

-Why are you here-

> *Matthew 19:4-6 (NIV), "'Haven't you read," he replied, "that at the beginning the Creator 'made them male and female,' and said, 'For this reason a man will leave his father and mother and be united to his wife, and the two will become one flesh'? So they are no longer two, but one flesh. Therefore what God has joined together, let no one separate.'"*

There are times in life when people step into roles and believe that their new position grants them some level of greater privilege and respect. This can happen in families when a daughter grows old enough to accept a marriage proposal from her boyfriend. Unless there are clearly spoken words among the parents and the children, the person with the perceived privilege will begin to walk in spaces that they believe are meant for them to join in because of a new deeper sense of belonging. Sometimes the lines of separation are blurred; where do the parents' roles end, and where does the fiancé's role begin? Unfortunately, many families are unclear about the boundaries, and this can bring conflict among everyone in both families. If the situation isn't handled with clear communication and a healthy understanding of the difference between being responsible *for* a person and being responsible *to* a person, what was once a promising new beginning can quickly become a tragic ending.

I once knew a man who asked his girlfriend to become his wife, but sadly they never made it to the altar. There were many things that contributed to this unhappy ending. In fact, so many things that I couldn't begin to share them all. However, the main contributing factor was the bride's parents' unwillingness to let go of their daughter, coupled with the bride not knowing that she was to stand by her husband and not her parents. Who am I responsible *for* and who am I responsible *to* are very important considerations especially when marriage is on the table. For this particular couple, things began to go wrong when the woman was diagnosed with a brain tumor. She had just gotten her first real job, one that offered perks which included a high-end insurance plan. However, because of the timing of the new job, the new insurance plan, and the brain tumor diagnosis; the insurance provider rejected any financial responsibility citing a pre-existing illness.

Everyone knew that the woman had been on her parent's insurance plan until just recently, everybody, that is, but the new insurance company. With a little investigation, the pre-existing illness claim would have been dropped, and the much-needed operation would have been covered. The problem here was two-fold. First, how long would it take for the insurance company to correct this so-called false claim through their bureaucracy so the operation could be scheduled? Second, the parents who previously were unwilling to let go of their daughter were suddenly more willing to wait for the insurance company to sort out the mix-up and less willing to do whatever was necessary to get their daughter the operation she needed. The fiancé was deeply troubled by the whole situation. He told his fiancé that he would make payments to the hospital if that was what was necessary to ensure she could have the tumor removed as quickly as possible.

The operation was scheduled and the doctor stated that the woman would probably need to remain in the hospital for 10-12 days after the surgery before she would be well enough to return home. Her fiancé took the time off from work to be by her side. As he put it, "I had never been more scared in my life. If something had happened and I wasn't there, I don't know how I would be able to forgive myself." The operation was completed and according to the doctor it was a success. The tumor had been removed. However, while sitting in the waiting room during the surgery, the fiancé and his soon to be in-laws didn't seem to be on the same team. They didn't appear to come together as one would expect a family would during such a crisis. Perhaps the parents were upset or embarrassed that they didn't put their daughters' needs above their own, due to the severity of the operation, by choosing to wait for the insurance company to sort out the mix-up instead of doing what their daughter's fiancé did, which was to act. The fiancé took notice, and a wedge began to form between them.

To make things worse, when the woman woke up from surgery and could begin to have visitors, she rejected her fiancé, asking him to leave. He was deeply wounded and hurt and didn't understand what was happening. He went to the hospital every day, sitting in the waiting room, hoping that his fiancé would rescind her rejection of him. On the fifth day, his soon to be in-laws stopped by the waiting room and asked, "Why are you here? You should just go home." Already wounded and feeling rejected, this statement sent the man into a confused depression. He thought, "How is it possible that all of this is happening? I feel that I have more right to be here than my fiancé's parents. We are engaged to be married. She is going to be my wife, for God's sake." The woman eventually returned home, but her relationship with her fiancé was vastly different. They were almost like two people who didn't know each other, almost like strangers. This went on for a few months, as the man didn't want to upset his fiancé, believing that she just needed time to heal from her surgery physically, spiritually, and emotionally.

> *Ephesians 4:2-3 (NIV), "Be completely humble and gentle; be patient, bearing with one another in love. Make every effort to keep the unity of the Spirit through the bond of peace."*

A few months had passed when, yet another emergency occurred in the family that the man was to marry into. The father had suffered a heart attack and needed triple by-pass surgery. After the doctors successfully performed the by-pass, the family began to visit him in the hospital. The couple who was to be married went to visit him as well. But the weirdest thing happened just before they left. The mother took her daughter's fiancé out into the hallway and said, "Now I know how you must have felt when my daughter was in the hospital."

Shocked, the man answered, "Now you know! Your daughter had her head carved into by a surgeon to remove a tumor from her brain, and now you know?" He thought to himself, "What the hell is wrong with this person?" But suddenly everything he didn't understand made sense, and yet it still didn't make any sense. He knew he wasn't crazy, but clearly this family had some odd thoughts about what was appropriate and what was not. Shortly thereafter, the man and his fiancé called off their marriage and went their separate ways.

When I heard this story, I thought, "How tragic." In the end, it was probably better that they didn't get married. Between the parent's over-involvement, and the engaged couples' inability to establish their commitment to each other, this couple probably had too much to overcome to be able to have a successful, fruitful marriage. However, the thing that stood out most to me, about this story, was the lack of awareness for the needs of other people. When the man shared the story, he never stated that an apology was offered by anyone, ever. This family didn't know the 12 most important words, and they obviously didn't know how and when to share them. The 12 most important words provide evidence that we see the other person, we hear the other person, and we value the other person.

Never speaking the words, I was wrong, I am sorry, please forgive me, I love you, fundamentally says, "You are not a priority to me." *Never* speaking the words also scars people with the insensitive question, "Why are you here?"

-Standing or running-

I have had the privilege of praying with many people over the years. Often, those I pray with are complete strangers. They will approach me at church and ask me to pray for countless desires. The circumstances I hear about are sometimes tragic, filled with pain and grief. Sometimes they are filled with remorse and guilt. Sometimes they are lost, desperately looking for direction. And sometimes, they are confused and don't know what to do. In a way that can only be explained by God's sovereignty, I often have personal experiences that line up with a prayer request or have helped another person through something similar. Both intangible assets allow me to provide a Spirit-filled prayer to the person seeking peace and hope. God weaves us together in such interesting ways.

While writing this book, one such prayer request came along. A man approached me after a church service and said he needed guidance concerning his daughter. So, I asked him to elaborate so I could pray more personally and intentionally. He said that he and his daughter were estranged, and he didn't know how or what to do next. I asked him for more clarification.

I asked, "How long have you been estranged? What is the reason for the conflict? Was it a series of small things that led to bigger problems? Or was it one huge fight?" Then I followed with, "You don't have to tell me what you are not comfortable sharing. However, I can see that you are clearly concerned, and this separation has caused you deep pain. I am simply trying to be more direct in my prayer."

He replied, "Everything you said, and more. I have been thinking about her more and more lately. She was once caught up in drugs and alcohol and I didn't know how to talk to her, nor did I know how to help her."

I asked, "Have you ever shared the 12 most important words with her before?"

He questioned, "What are the 12 most important words?"

"I was wrong. I am sorry. Please forgive me. I love you," I replied.

He indicated, "I have never shared those words with her before."

I said, "Sir, I have had a similar situation with one of my children in the past. God prompted me to run after my son. By His grace, I listened and responded. I am in the process of writing a book and I just included that part of our journey in it. Sometimes we are standing and sometimes we are running, and you need to know the difference."

He asked, "How do I know when to stand and when to run?"

That's when I shared these scriptures with him.

> *Luke 15:20-24 (NIV), 'So he got up and went to his father. "But while he was still a long way off, his father saw him and was filled with compassion for him; he ran to his son, threw his arms around him and kissed him." "The son said to him, 'Father, I have sinned against heaven and against you. I am no longer worthy to be called your son.'" "But the father said to his servants, 'Quick! Bring the best robe and put it on him. Put a ring on his finger and sandals on his feet. Bring the fattened calf and kill it. Let's have a feast and celebrate. For this son of mine was dead and is alive again; he was lost and is found.'" So they began to celebrate.'*

> *Luke 15:3-7 (NIV), 'Then Jesus told them this parable: "Suppose one of you has a hundred sheep and loses one of them. Doesn't he leave the ninety-nine in the open country and go after the lost sheep until he finds it? And when he finds it, he joyfully puts it on his shoulders and goes home. Then he calls his friends and neighbors together and says, 'Rejoice with me; I have found my lost sheep.' I tell you that in the same way there will be more rejoicing in heaven over one sinner who repents than over ninety-nine righteous persons who do not need to repent.'"*

I followed by saying, "The same Father that stands vigilant waiting for His son is also the same Father that leaves the 99 and runs after the *one*. If you are uncertain of which to do, my suggestion is to *always* lean towards running after the *one*. That is something we all desire from our Heavenly Father. We all want to be seen, heard, and valued. God calls us to love others in the same way that he loves us. When God prompted me to run after my son, amazing blessings began to happen in our relationship. Those blessings can happen for you and your daughter as well. But please remember to share the 12 most important words with her. Nothing says I see you; I hear you; and I value you; like taking *complete* responsibility for the conflict between you by sharing these words, 'I was wrong. I am sorry. Please forgive me. I love you.' These 12 powerful words will assure your daughter that nothing else matters but your relationship with her. Nothing!" At this, the man's eyes were filled with tears for his daughter. I was so grateful that God gave me something of value to share with him at just the right time. I also knew that a man and his daughter were going to have a long-awaited reunion because we serve a mighty God.

-When lies become truth-

One of the worst things that can happen in this life is the dismantling of the family unit. For some reason, segments of our culture have a romance with recreating what God has already established. That's not to say that those who are walking with Jesus aren't making this romance more enticing by our lack of commitment to our spouses when we get married. We see divorce rates climbing to new levels, almost yearly, and this includes those both in and out of the Church. If we look deep enough at this dilemma, we find it's not a divorce problem we have. No! It's a commitment problem. And this only serves as fuel for those who want to destroy what they seem to despise, God's plan for life.

> *Mark 10:6-9 (NIV), "But at the beginning of creation God 'made them male and female.' 'For this reason a man will leave his father and mother and be united to his wife, and the two will become one flesh.' So they are no longer two, but one flesh. Therefore what God has joined together, let no one separate."*

> *Proverbs 31:10-11 (NIV), "A wife of noble character who can find? She is worth far more than rubies. Her husband has full confidence in her and lacks nothing of value."*

> *Titus 1:6-7 (NIV), "An elder must be blameless, faithful to his wife, a man whose children believe and are not open to the charge of being wild and disobedient. Since an overseer manages God's household, he must be blameless—not overbearing, not quick-tempered, not given to drunkenness, not violent, not pursuing dishonest gain."*

> *Psalm 127:3 (NIV), "Children are a heritage from the Lord, offspring a reward from him."*
>
> *Proverbs 22:6 (NIV), "Start children off on the way they should go, and even when they are old they will not turn from it."*

I know many men who have found themselves in the deep murky waters of divorce. Most of us don't handle these situations well because they tear at our emotions and bring untold levels of hurt and pain. Where children are involved, divorce becomes even more deadly as it places every member of the family in uncharted waters and can destroy relationships that were once sure and solid. All it takes for calamity to happen is for the parent(s) to allow their emotions to be the driving force behind their decision making when the divorce begins. This behavior, left at the helm for even a few short days, provides more than enough of a wedge for this process to begin to run its course. Once the storm begins, it's almost impossible to control the direction of the relationships moving forward.

One of the men that I mentor started down this road of devastation and didn't know how to stop it. Like all humans, he was hurt and is still healing because of the rejection and confusion that divorce causes. Again, when children are involved, divorce becomes very complicated. He and his ex-wife didn't see the needs of their children as a priority as they were too busy grasping for whatever life source they could hold onto themselves. Their children remained living with his ex-wife. Two things ensued that brought about the erosion and eventual breakdown of his relationship with his children. Remember, all it takes is a lapse in judgment, sitting in your own pain, for even a few days to bring about disaster in our relationships.

First, his ex-wife didn't see the need for their children to ever see their father. They became pawns to leverage her rage and anger against her ex-husband. Unfortunately, this practice of using the children as leverage is all too common in divorce situations. She went as far as to influence her children to believe that their father was no good, didn't care for them, and didn't love them anymore. Being the child in a divorce is a confusing place to be, especially if the environment isn't nurturing from all sides. Children want to grasp onto whatever life source they can just as much as, if not more than, the parent. Having been in this situation myself many times during my childhood, I can attest to this scary predicament.

Second, and what most likely made this situation worse, was the father's lack of connection with his children. What started out as limited, quickly eroded to birthdays and Christmas only, and eventually became essentially non-existent. In his defense, he was dealing with his own pain, caught in his own thoughts of failure, and wasn't strong enough to endure his children's rejection or override their mother's constant reminders that he was a horrible father. Remember, divorce is a very complicated thing. Parents who enter this domain must take every possible avenue of making themselves healthy in every way including spiritually, physically, and emotionally *so that* they can be available to their children and support their every need.

When I met this man and began trying to help him unravel the web of brokenness that he was in, I remember him desperately wanting to establish a strong bond with his children. Whenever he reached out to them with a text message or a phone call he wasn't received favorably. Rarely did his children even reply. If he stopped by their house, many times they weren't home or didn't want to see him. The rejection took its toll on him, and he was distraught, maybe even depressed. This left him not wanting to approach his children for fear of further rejection. I have often reminded him that this is when lies become truth. The lies his ex-wife instilled in their children's minds about him have now taken root as truth due to his absence. What a horrible place to be for all involved.

I can't help but think about how this marriage might have been saved by sharing the 12 most important words at pivotal moments along the way. I can't help but think about how this man's relationship with his children may have been saved, even though divorce happened, by sharing the 12 most important words at crucial moments. This is a tragic story, and I have no doubt there are many more like it across the world. The power we hold in 12 little words, four short phrases, is unlimited. However, until we learn to use them "in the *quick*" with humble sincerity will we ever see that power ourselves. Our relationships are dying all around us. Will we take action, or will we continue to fall victim to brokenness? 12 words could make all the difference in the world.

> *1 Peter 4:8 (NIV), "Above all, love each other deeply, because love covers over a multitude of sins."*

Jeff Frick

-My way or the highway-

I often receive calls from complete strangers who have been given my number from a mutual friend. They call for various reasons, but the most common is that they have a problem they don't know how to solve, or they have a situation they don't know how to navigate. In the fall of 2020, my family and I were in Oregon for my eldest son's wedding. We were there for five days and during those five days I received multiple calls from people who were in some kind of predicament. One of those calls came from a man who was having trouble communicating with his son and needed guidance. When he called and tried to explain his situation, I knew right away that it would require more time than a 20 to 30-minute conversation. So, I suggested that I call him back when I returned home. He agreed.

When I returned home, I called the man the following day. He said that he and his son were not communicating, and he wanted to know how he could get his son to listen to him. I asked him if he knew what started the conflict. He said, "Yes! I threw him out of my house."

I replied, "You threw him out of your house? Can I ask why?"

He stated, "I told him I wanted him to go to college and he had decided that he is not going to honor my wishes. So, I threw him out."

I asked, "What is he doing with his life? Is he working?"

He said, "Yes. He is a district manager at Taco Bell."

I said, "Well, it doesn't sound like he is a bum. He has what I would consider a good job."

The man said, "My son didn't follow my directions. In *my* house it *will* be *my* way. If you don't do what *I* want in *my* house, the door *will* catch you on the ass on the way out. Period!"

At this, I changed course and asked him, "How do you plan to get your son back now that you threw him out? It appears that getting your way has cost you a close relationship with your son. Is that what you wanted to happen?"

He repeated, "My son didn't go to college. It was my desire that he go to college. He disobeyed me, so it had to be this way."

I asked him, "What about your son's plans? Does he have a say in what his future looks like? Or does he have to do exactly what you want him to do? I am not sure that I would call that parenting."

He replied again, "I will say it again, he didn't do what I wanted him to do. That's that!"

I said, "Sir, you have called me because you apparently want to have a relationship with your son that is both communicative and intimate. But if he must do everything your way, he most likely *isn't* coming back. You have basically told him that he doesn't measure up and that his plans are worthless. Have you thought about sharing the 12 most important words with him?"

He said, "I don't know what the 12 most important words are."

"I was wrong. I am sorry. Please forgive me. I love you," I replied.

He said, "But I am not wrong! You don't understand. I have worked hard my whole life. I have built companies and created vast sums of money. I am a millionaire, and I want him to follow in my footsteps."

I told him, "Your son is not going to come back until he can stand shoulder to shoulder with you. You told him that he doesn't measure up, he isn't enough, all because he didn't do it your way. Your son has been challenged, and he won't return until he amasses the fortune that you have or has more than you have. He won't return until he proves you wrong."

That's when the man became worried and scared. He said, "I don't want that to happen."

I told him, "It's too late, the damage has already been done. You laid the gauntlet down and you threw him out."

That's when the man asked, "Would you talk to my son."

I stated, "I can't force my way into your son's life any more than you can."

He said, "What if I was to convince him to talk to you?"

I replied, "You both need to be present to solve this issue. This is not a 'him' problem or a 'you' problem. This is a 'both of you' problem. If you can get your son to come to my office with you, we may have a chance of straightening things out. But I can't guarantee anything because both people have to be willing to do their part."

That's when the man displayed his true colors, and I knew the problem with his son would haunt him forever. The man asked, "What do you charge?"

To which I responded, "Nothing. I never take money from people."

This infuriated the man, and he screamed, "In this house we don't do #*^%ing charity! You got that!"

I cautiously responded, "Sir, I can see you are a proud man. And it appears you like to pay your way through life. Kindness is not something you respond to. So, the price is still zero. However, you are free to make a donation of any amount at any time to my ministry."

At this he said, "Well alright then!" and he hung up.

I never heard from him again. I feel sorry that his son must perform to his father's liking in order to receive his father's love. Which of course is not love, favor maybe, but definitely not love.

> Luke 6:43-45 (NIV), "No good tree bears bad fruit, nor does a bad tree bear good fruit. Each tree is recognized by its own fruit. People do not pick figs from thornbushes, or grapes from briers. A good man brings good things out of the good stored up in his heart, and an evil man brings evil things out of the evil stored up in his heart. For the mouth speaks what the heart is full of."

-It's your fault-

In addition to the men that I mentor, I often find myself sitting in front of couples who are struggling in their relationship. The couples usually don't come together when they first begin to explore how to solve their problems. Typically, I am sitting with the husband, and he is hoping that I will endorse whatever bad behaviors he has demonstrated that contributed to the problems in his marriage. What every man quickly finds out after spending time with me is that I will never fully endorse his story knowing that there are three sides to every story: his, hers and the truth. One of the promises that I outlined in my first book, "How do I Love my *Neighbor*, 4 PROMISES AND 6 TRUTHS" is that I will never be your "Yes" man. That is something that I live by.

After a husband realizes that I will not grant him the easy pass that he desperately seeks, he will sometimes bring his wife with him to explore what options there are to find resolution and wholeness. Unfortunately, most couples wait until their problems are so severe that it would literally take an act of God to bring restoration and healing in their marriage. I never sit alone with a woman, but I have taken phone calls from time to time when they reach out with huge concerns for how to bring an end to the conflict in their marriage. One particular couple that I have known for many years was having great difficulty in their marriage. They did what most couples do, they waited too long.

First the wife called me. She said that her marital problems were so bad, that she and her husband were living in separate houses. They had to navigate work schedules and the children they shared, which is why they could not make a permanent separation at that time. So, I asked what had happened and how I might be able to help. She indicated that her husband had been unfaithful, by violating the covenant of their marriage, and takes no responsibility for his actions. Side note: I have fielded more than a dozen of these types of calls through the years. Most of the women who call want to keep their marriage strong but wonder how they will ever be able to forgive their husbands. I remind these women that it is honorable that they want to redeem their marriages, and that God would want them to do so as well. However, if they were truly seeking restoration, at some point they will need to forgive their husbands. It may take some time to do so, but if their marriage is ever going to survive, the wife cannot use the infidelity as leverage to get what she wants when things don't go her way. I shared those views with the woman on the phone. All she could say is this, "It's his fault!"

Romans 14:12 (NIV), "So then, each of us will give an account of ourselves to God."

Jeff Frick

At this point she went into a long discourse about the history of their dysfunction and why it was her husband's fault. She then asked if I would reach out to him and talk to him to see if there was anything that could be done to redirect the course they were on. I agreed to her request. A few days later, her husband arrived at my office, and we began attempting to drill down to the root of their problems. The first question I asked was why he broke his covenant with his wife. Just as his wife did, he shared an extremely long but shallow history of the dysfunction of their marriage.

That's when I asked the same question but in a more investigative manner, "None of that explains why you broke the covenant of marriage. I need to know what drove you to do something so severe. Why did you break your covenant?" That's when he said something that I didn't expect to hear.

He said, "She cheated first! It's her fault!"

I questioned, "What? Wait a minute. You mean to tell me that she cheated on you? She said that you cheated on her?"

He said, "I did cheat, but only after she cheated first. She takes no responsibility for this mess and blames me for everything. I am the innocent one!" That's when I reminded him that by cheating, he made himself the same as his wife. He has no moral high ground to stand on. There is no virtue in what he has done.

> *Proverbs 16:25 (NIV), "There is a way that appears to be right, but in the end it leads to death."*

Imagine how differently this story could have played out if this couple would have shared the 12 most important words at various times throughout their marriage. It was clear to me that they didn't share the 12 most important words, because they didn't even know what the 12 most important words were. Hopefully today they know what those words are. However, if you intend to share the 12 most important words, you *must* be willing to take responsibility for your actions. Clearly, neither of them was willing to take *any* responsibility for their actions. Both the husband and the wife violated the covenant of marriage, and each blames the other person. I can't help but think about the misery their children face as they navigate the horrors of divorce all because two grown adults were unwilling to share the 12 most important words a few times along the way and instead placed all the blame on someone else. How very sad.

-Complete loss of control-

There are times when we are walking through life with certainty and clear direction. Our circumstances, no matter how crazy, don't dictate our demeanor, and we exhibit love, joy, peace, patience, kindness, goodness, faithfulness, gentleness, and self-control. And sadly, there are times when we aren't able to exhibit any aspect of self-control. What's the difference? When we are walking in control, we are walking in the Spirit that God implants into our souls when we said "yes" to Jesus as Lord and Savior. The times we lose control, we have allowed our flesh, our feelings, our sinful nature, and the world to dominate our behavior. One is good for us and those around us, while the other is never good for anyone.

> *Galatians 5:22-25 (NIV), "But the fruit of the Spirit is love, joy, peace, forbearance, kindness, goodness, faithfulness, gentleness and self-control. Against such things there is no law. Those who belong to Christ Jesus have crucified the flesh with its passions and desires. Since we live by the Spirit, let us keep in step with the Spirit."*

Around 15 years old, my son Michael's behavior began to change. In this season, I thought I did a pretty good job of walking in self-control most of the time. He and I would have many conversations about why it was important to surround ourselves with people that we trust, people that have our best interests at heart, and people who will always steer us in the right direction. I remember during one of our conversations, Michael said, "Dad, why do you always think the worst is going to happen to me? You seem to believe that I will do something that I won't be able to recover from. You have shared with me and my brothers all the crazy things you did as a kid, and you turned out all right."

That's when I quickly shared, "Michael, I want you to know that I have been on this planet much longer than you have. I have wisdom that you have yet to attain. When behaviors begin to change negatively instead of positively, we are headed in the wrong direction. I shared the stories from my youth with you and your brothers for a couple of reasons. First, I wanted you to know that I *have* made mistakes. We *all* make mistakes. It's *okay* to make mistakes. But the greatest mistake is not learning from the previous mistake and then not changing our behavior, so we don't repeat the same mistake again. Second, I wanted you and your brothers to know that I have walked in your shoes. I was once young, and I understand that you will learn some things the *hard* way. I know that I cannot prevent your every curiosity because mistakes are how we learn and grow in this life. However, more important than anything else, you seem to have used my life as the mark of excellence to achieve for yourself. I am telling you right now, if I am your mark, you have set the bar way too low. I want so much more for you than you even want for yourself."

When Michael was 17 years old, he decided that he didn't want to live in our house anymore, as the rules were just too much for him. He was screaming and yelling that he was packing his things and leaving. I remember my wife began to cry and that was enough for Michael to reconsider his threats. After he and my wife shared a long embrace, he rushed over to me and screamed, "I have decided I am staying. I am staying for them, but I am not staying for you. Make no mistake, I hate you!"

The Holy Spirit left me speechless in this moment. No hair stood up on my head, nor did feelings of rejection overwhelm me, nor did anger overcome me because of the disrespect from my son toward me. Instead, I embraced my son and said, "Michael, I love you. I would rather you hate me and have a life, than not hate me and have no life because you are caught in this world. You are my son. We are going to continue to do things that families do, and you will be a part of every one of those moments. I am grateful that you have decided to stay. This will always be your home, and you will always be welcomed here." I am still amazed today when I think about how that moment played out. I have no idea how I was able to keep my wits about me as only the Holy Spirit could make such things possible.

> *Galatians 5:16-18 (NIV), "So I say, walk by the Spirit, and you will not gratify the desires of the flesh. For the flesh desires what is contrary to the Spirit, and the Spirit what is contrary to the flesh. They are in conflict with each other, so that you are not to do whatever you want. But if you are led by the Spirit, you are not under the law."*

Then came the night, a few years later, when everything changed. Michael had been gone for over three weeks. It was not unusual for him to be gone for weeks at a time. In fact, it happened so often that we quit thinking about calling in a "missing persons" request to the police. We never knew where he was because he would turn off his "location services" on his phone. When he entered our home that night, he was angry at my wife and me. He spoke at length about all the things that were wrong in his life and how angry he was at us because we had been the cause of them all.

We listened to his entire tirade and then I said, "Michael, you are angry at us? For what? Are you angry because we tried to give you a good life? Are you angry because we tried to keep you from the dangers of this world? Are you angry because we love you even when you are disrespectful? Are you angry because we continue to live in fear and worry because we don't know where you are? You are angry at us?" To this point, I was still in control. But something in me snapped. I don't know what happened, but for the next few minutes I went on a rampage of terror and Michael was my victim. I lost complete control.

I don't remember exactly what I said because I was not in my right mind, but I do remember starting my tirade with, "You don't know what anger is." From there everything went blank. I started yelling, which turned to screaming, which turned to nearly assaulting him. Michael sat there and listened to it all, as did my wife. Neither of them interrupted me. In the end, I lost complete control of myself, and my son was the recipient of something he should have never had to endure, especially not from his father. My childish outburst ended when I tore a muscle in my chest which left me bedridden for five days. I don't know if I would have stopped screaming at Michael had it not been for the torn muscle. While I laid in my bed, my right mind returned, many thoughts came over me. I contemplated, "I never apologized for my eruption. I never told Michael 'I was wrong' and that 'I am sorry.' What have I done? How will we ever recover from this? Will I ever have a meaningful relationship with Michael again?"

Proverbs 25:28 (NIV), "Like a city whose walls are broken through is a person who lacks self-control."

Jeff Frick

(Sketch by Steve Perucca)

Proverbs 4:23 (NIV)
"Above all else, guard your heart, for everything you do flows from it."

2

I Was Wrong

"You can't go back and change the beginning, but you can start where you are and change the ending."
-C.S. Lewis

---

1 John 1:8 (NIV), "If we claim to be without sin, we deceive ourselves and the truth is not in us."

Have you ever wondered why it is so difficult for most people to be able to say the words; "I was wrong?" Far too many people will never say these three simple words because in their minds, they are right and everyone else must be wrong. Let me paint a picture for your mind's eye that conveys just how difficult it may be for some to utter the three simple words, "I was wrong." Imagine you are in your car traveling down the road when suddenly you find yourself in an accident and you are crashing into a body of water. What would be going through your mind? There would be an explosion inside of you. Undoubtedly the only thought occupying your mind would be getting out of the sinking car. All your thoughts would funnel into one focus: get out or drown. Without a doubt you would quickly spring into action doing anything and everything possible to escape from the sinking car. You would do anything to keep yourself alive, because if you don't, you will die.

The explosion inside of you in that instance is one of the characteristics of being human. Life must go on and we will do almost anything to preserve our lives. The only problem here is that we are not talking about our life being stripped from existence. We are talking about keeping a relationship thriving. But for some of us, saying the words, "I was wrong" literally kills us. We would never "give in" that easily, much like the fact that we wouldn't just allow ourselves to drown in the sinking car by doing nothing and ultimately conceding to death. When our proverbial car crashes into the water, the person on the receiving end of our foolishness and subsequent deflection, often feel as if they've gone twelve rounds in the boxing ring with Mike Tyson. We would rather allow pain to be inflicted upon another than to die to self. The really sad truth to this is that the other person is usually someone close to us who we claim to love and respect. The question is, why do we do this to each other? Why is our self-preservation more important than those we claim to love? We believe with all our hearts that we know how to love, but then we inflict pain because our love lacks sacrifice. Which by definition is not love.

How desperate and lonely must we be to spend our lives protecting and loving ourselves instead of loving those whom God placed in our lives? We are called to demonstrate His love. A truth that cannot be understated nor debated is this…what we have learned to receive from God is on full display in our every interaction, every day. How are we to demonstrate His love?

In my first book, "How do I Love my *Neighbor*? 4 PROMISES AND 6 TRUTHS," I share another simple truth that helps us answer this question: you cannot give what you do not have. We are wrong often, whether we choose to believe it or not. May we learn to express these simple words, "I was wrong," to save our relationships. This is far better than keeping those words silent, to save ourselves. When you are never wrong, you become a lonely person, and lonely people wrapped up in themselves make a very small package.

There is never a guarantee that saying the words "I was wrong" will bring us together and repair the pieces that we broke in the process; however, the humbling of our hearts will prove we took the wise route. Our broken relationships won't ever get any better until we humble ourselves and treat people the way that God treats us. If you have broken relationships, but don't know God because you think He's not real, or you believe you can manage just fine on your own, perhaps it's time to invest or reinvest in the One who can redeem and restore all things. All you must do is humble yourself. What are you waiting for?

-Only God-

I have a friend who has heard the words, "I was wrong," from the most unlikely source. Hearing the words didn't bring wholeness to his relationship from which the words originated, but it did bring peace in the middle of hostility. I met my friend when he was in the early stages of an impending divorce. Like many divorces, it was evident that anger, frustration, cursing, blaming, and even using the children like pawns to gain leverage was on display. I asked my friend if he was willing to try something different. His reply was simple, "I'll do anything to save my marriage." I told him that what I was asking him to do may not necessarily save his marriage, but it would provide something for his children that they desperately needed.

I asked my friend to make two promises. These promises were to his children, himself, and to me. First, I asked him to be willing to become something that he currently was not for the benefit of his children. Second, I asked him to stop using negative words to describe his wife no matter what. Furthermore, if the final outcome was that she was to become his ex-wife, he still had to keep the promise of not using negative words to describe her. He asked me why he was making these promises. I told him that I had lived in his children's shoes. I had experienced living in brokenness as a child because of my parent's multiple divorces. I believed my experience could help him have an outcome that was different from the vast majority of kids who are products of divorce. My personal experiences could make things vastly different for his children. He knew holding true to these promises would require much effort, yet he eagerly agreed.

To become something that he currently was not would require him to press into Jesus in an entirely new way. I reminded him that I would hold him accountable for the promises he had made to himself, his children, and to me. He quickly surrounded himself with men who did the same and were going through similar situations. When he asked me why it was necessary to press into Jesus like never before, I explained to him that we don't stop sinning by trying to stop sinning. **We stop sinning by devoting ourselves to Jesus.** You won't become a better dad by trying to be a better dad. You will become a better dad by devoting yourself to Jesus and inviting Him alongside you as you journey through parenthood. I gently explained to my friend that his children's lives had become chaotic and more broken than he could fathom and that he would need to be the calm that they could count on.

With Jesus, his children would begin to experience peace in the brokenness and feel calm in the chaos even if it were for short periods of time. With Jesus, his children would always have something tangible to hold onto. I shared with him that as a child of divorce myself, my experiences could have been much different and so much better if one of my parents had been able to be the calm in the chaos that would give the sense of peace amongst the brokenness in our home. This would be a huge undertaking considering all the emotions that come with divorce, both for the children and the adults.

The second promise proved to be just as difficult. Not speaking negatively about his wife to anyone even if she became his ex-wife at some point was another promise meant solely for his children's benefit. I told my friend that if he spoke a negative word about his wife to anyone at any time, he would eventually speak those negative words about her in front of their children. He would then be taking part in using his children as pawns to gain leverage. Having experienced that as a child myself, I informed my friend that he would be placing his children in the uncomfortable, and impossible, position of having to choose between their parents. If he was going to be the calm, safe place for his children, he would have to control his emotions on every level. This would require more of his surrender to Jesus Christ.

> *Philippians 2:5-11 (NIV), "In your relationships with one another, have the same mindset as Christ Jesus: Who, being in very nature God did not consider equality with God something to be used to his own advantage; rather, he made himself nothing by taking the very nature of a servant, being made in human likeness. And being found in appearance as a man, he humbled himself by becoming obedient to death—even death on a cross! Therefore God exalted him to the highest place and gave him the name that is above every name, that at the name of Jesus every knee should bow, in heaven and on earth and under the earth, and every tongue acknowledge that Jesus Christ is Lord, to the glory of God the Father."*

Since he was taking my suggestions and the promises he made seriously, he would ask me to read and "approve" many of the text messages he had drafted that were meant for his wife. Very seldom did I approve of the messages that he wanted to use as a response. Honestly, I cannot remember a single message that I did not ask him to re-write, as I am not willing to be anyone's "yes" man. Eventually his wife became his ex-wife. The season of impending divorce eventually gave way to a brutal divorce that was taxing on him, his children, and his family. However, he never stopped devoting himself to Jesus. Every now and again, God gave him a blessing that he could hold onto like a compass that let him know that he was headed in the right direction.

The Twelve Most Important Words

Eventually, the rigidity of the rules laid down by the court system softened. Not because of the court, but because his relationship with his ex-wife began to flourish. While they learned how to grow, communicate with one another, and work together in this new dynamic as co-parents, his time with his children became more plentiful, easy going, and not so rules based. His ex-wife became more pleasant, and communication was easier. Did something happen? Yes! His devotion to Jesus began to plant seeds of change in the heart of his ex-wife. She could see, maybe for the first time, that her children needed to be with their dad as often as they were with her and that parenting their children would be far more beneficial together than separate. It was not about them, but about what was best for their children they were raising together, but in separate homes.

This new change of behavior continued to evolve between my friend and his ex-wife for the next few years. His children were flourishing in this new environment in a way that only God could have orchestrated. But He wasn't finished yet. There came a time when his ex-wife was having major difficulties in her new marriage. Her marital problems continued to grow until one night she showed up at his front door unannounced. He invited her in, and she stayed in their daughter's room for three days. He waited patiently for her to shed some light on why she chose to take refuge in his house, of all places. When she was ready to return home, she told him that her husband had been verbally and physically abusive and that she needed to leave. Let's pause to reflect on the gravity of what took place during these three days. His ex-wife needed to take refuge from an abusive situation, in which she didn't call her parents, she didn't call her siblings, she didn't even call any of her friends. Instead, she called her ex-husband who had endured an ugly divorce he didn't want; yet opened the door and allowed her to stay in his home, providing her a safe place during her personal storm. Why? One answer…Jesus!

A few months passed and the same thing happened again. His ex-wife showed up on his doorstep and stayed a few days because she needed refuge during her storm. This time, he said to her, "We need to see how to get you some different help." They had many conversations over the next few days, but none was more telling than when she shared the words, "*I was wrong*" with him. "*I was wrong*" are some of the most difficult words to ever escape our lips. Even though a divorce occurred, and frustrations lingered for a number of years, those difficult words were shared. I watched my friend grow in the Lord and many people witnessed miracles. Only God can do such things. Thanks be to God!

Jeff Frick

-It almost didn't happen-

I was nearly finished writing my second book, "IDENTITY MATTERS- The Power of BELONGING," and I felt prompted to include one additional review. I reached out to my friend Dave and asked if he would be inclined to help me with this endeavor. I asked Dave because he is well spoken, highly intelligent, and he knows the Lord Jesus Christ. Thankfully, he agreed and said he would be in touch soon. I was expecting Dave's review to be sent via email, so I was surprised when I got a call from him instead. Dave gave me some very insightful and important feedback. However, he told me that he was not going to write a review. He shared with me that I was most likely going to be sued for writing the book, and in his opinion, I should not go through with publishing it. When asked why he felt so strongly about me not having my book published, he first said that I had taken some photos off the Internet and that I would most likely have copyright issues. Next, he told me that I had named members of my family and that I would most likely be sued for libel, defamation, and slander.

I was a bit shocked. This was not what I thought I was going to hear when asking Dave for his thoughts regarding my book. I didn't understand the legalities of what Dave was explaining to me. So, I asked, "How does a person go about sharing their personal stories while dodging legal ramifications?"

He said that naming people is never a good idea. I told him that I had originally written the book without names, however, the people who were helping me edit the book said that they could not follow what was happening and needed names to understand and make sense of what they were reading. My parents married each other and then after divorcing were both married two more times to other people. Without names, it would be nearly impossible to write the chapters that shared my story.

I asked Dave how would anyone ever tell their own story if they cannot include names of the people in their own family? Dave told me that he didn't read the whole book but indicated that in Chapter 3 I had written about my son Michael, who had passed away. Dave told me that I had many interesting things to say about my son and that I should write a book about him. But Dave also indicated that he probably wouldn't read that book either because he has a son that is struggling and depressed and it would be far too emotional for him. He said that he and his wife almost lost their son more than once. He said that he had been on a cliff of desperation with his son too many times and never wanted to visit that place again. I told Dave that if God tells me to write a book about Michael, that I would do it. However, the book that I was currently writing was the book I felt that God had asked me to write, and I was going to finish it. I thanked Dave for his insight.

> *Ecclesiastes 11:5 (NIV), "As you do not know the path of the wind, or how the body is formed in a mother's womb, so you cannot understand the work of God, the Maker of all things."*

After publishing my first book, "How Do I Love my *Neighbor*? 4 PROMISES AND 6 TRUTHS," nearly nine months passed before I was able to record it for audio distribution. However, after publishing my second book, only five weeks passed before I was able to record it for audio distribution. When I walked into the studio, I was overly surprised to find Dave's son sitting in the lead chair of the recording studio. This was the son that Dave was so emotional about when he spoke to me on the phone a few weeks earlier. The work of recording the book lasted three days, a day longer than any of us had anticipated. During the recording process, Dave's son made everything pleasant and easy. He was professional, inviting, calm, cool, and a real delight to work with. In fact, we bonded over the three days, and we hoped to be able to work together on the book that you are reading right now.

When the recording was completed, Dave reached out to me. He was filled with joy as he told me how his son had been so excited and filled with joy over the past three days of recording with me. Dave said, "I don't know how to thank you. My son felt appreciated. My son was loved. My son was given purpose. My son felt like he was included. My son felt like he mattered to people. My son read your book over the past three days as you were recording it, and the Gospel was shared with him. You have no idea what this experience meant to him. You have no idea what this experience means to me. I can't thank you enough!"

I responded, "Dave, you are very welcome. I am glad that your son was in the studio. I am grateful for the opportunity to have worked with him and to bond with him. But I have to tell you, Dave, you didn't want me to publish or record this book. If I had listened to you instead of God, this entire experience would not have happened. If writing and recording this book was only for the purpose of providing this experience for your son, was it worth it?"

Dave replied, "I was wrong. Yes! Yes, it was definitely worth it!"

-Not willing to wait any longer-

Sometimes we are blind to the things that are important to other people around us. Because we are sometimes blind to what others value and hold dear, we also cannot understand why our relationships are eroding right in front of us. For many of us, we are giving love and affection to those we love, but somehow it doesn't seem to be enough, and we are left scratching our heads and racking our brains, wondering what we aren't doing since it seems like we are doing everything we think we should. Why do our relationships crumble even though we are offering our best? We can come up with multiple reasons for this quandary, but we can filter all our reasons down to one common cause; what *we want* to give versus what *they need*. **There is a vast difference between giving someone what I want them to have versus finding out what they need.** In fact, I would argue that giving someone what I want them to have, is the polar opposite of finding out what they need. If this is the first time you are hearing this, let it sink in and perhaps reread this paragraph.

If we give people what we want them to have and never find out what they need, we are not loving them, we are in fact dismissing them. In effect, our actions are saying, "You will take what I am offering and like it. I don't care what you think or even what you need. I am not willing to consider your interests at all. This is what I am willing to give you, like it or not." That sentiment seems rather harsh, because it is. The truth is, we are not attempting to convey such ugly words to our loved ones. We are trying in every way to love them. However, when we continually dismiss them, those unspoken words become their reality.

Every person on this planet needs three things from those closest to them: (1) to be seen, (2) to be heard, and (3) to be valued. When we give them what we want them to have and disregard what they need, we never really see them, hear them, or value them. And sometimes, the person we love actually grows cold toward us and is not willing to wait any longer for us to see them, hear them, or value them. That's when the relationship dissolves.

I minister to many men who are dealing with relationship issues that include infidelity, impending divorce, and all sorts of conflict in general. When they come to me for advice, it usually takes a few meetings to get to the root of their problem. Unfortunately, by the time most of the men I work with ask for help, the relationship is already in critical condition. What compounds the problem is that our culture is saturated with quick fixes and shortcut answers to everything. Due to this path of least resistance conditioning, most people are unfamiliar and ill-prepared to endure the hard work it will take to restore their relationship. Most men think they can solve their relationship issues with a book, a couple of classes, or a few well-placed buzz words spoken now and again. What they don't know and eventually come to find out, sometimes the hard way, is that they have not loved their loved one and must make major changes. If they don't change, the current relationship will break, and all future relationships will be subject to the same fate.

Jim came to see me for the first time because there was conflict in his marriage. We spoke in depth about his thoughts pertaining to his current situation and he shared all that he had been *doing* for his wife and daughter. Although he didn't understand why his relationship was suffering, he was determined to fix it. Eventually, he brought his wife with him, and we discussed their conflict from a different perspective. There is one question I always ask married couples who are in conflict: "Prior to marriage, did you receive any pre-marriage counseling?" The vast majority of these couples universally answer that they had not particpated in any type of pre-marriage counseling. This was also the case with the couple in front of me. After a few hours, with a few tools to put into practice, and a new deeper understanding of what marriage is and is not from God's perspective, both husband and wife seemed confident that they could move closer to the unity of one, designed by God.

Nearly three months passed before I saw Jim again. This time, he was extremely fearful and anxious that his marriage was in deep trouble. He couldn't understand what was happening and why his wife was so obstinate. Jim and I began to meet weekly from that time on. Over the next several weeks we dissected his marriage, his behaviors, and his wife's behaviors from his perspective because she was apparently no longer interested in finding common ground. Slowly, Jim began to see the error in his ways. With a genuine pursuit of God, Jim knew that he had not treated his wife appropriately. That is not to say that he abused her in any way, but Jim gave his wife what he wanted her to have and never thought to ask what she needed. As he learned how a husband is to love his wife through the lens of God, he attempted to make amends with her.

> *Ephesians 5:25-28 (NIV)*, *"Husbands, love your wives, just as Christ loved the church and gave himself up for her to make her holy, cleansing her by the washing with water through the word, and to present her to himself as a radiant church, without stain or wrinkle or any other blemish, but holy and blameless. In this same way, husbands ought to love their wives as their own bodies. He who loves his wife loves himself."*

Unfortunately for Jim, he had waited far too long to make the adjustments necessary to show his wife that she was important. Jim came back week after week hoping to gain something tangible that would keep the train on the tracks. I remember one such meeting when Jim was angry, frustrated, hurt, and confused. He said in the most painful voice, "Why is this happening? Why can't I stop it? All I ever do is work and golf."

I asked Jim these questions, "Would your wife or daughter ever consider asking you not to golf so that you might do something else with them? Or is your golf game off-limits, or taboo, and they know never to interfere?" Jim stared into the room with a blank face pondering the questions that I asked.

After a long pause, Jim responded, "I don't like the answer to your questions."

I responded, "Jim, that's why you are here. And that's why your wife is not willing to wait any longer for you to place her first."

Jim finally shared the words, "I was wrong." Unfortunately, he shared them with me. I don't know if he ever shared them with his wife.

-God is still with you-

> *1 Corinthians 9:19-23 (NIV)*, *"Though I am free and belong to no one, I have made myself a slave to everyone, to win as many as possible. To the Jews I became like a Jew, to win the Jews. To those under the law I became like one under the law (though*

I myself am not under the law), so as to win those under the law. To those not having the law I became like one not having the law (though I am not free from God's law but am under Christ's law), so as to win those not having the law. To the weak I became weak, to win the weak. I have become all things to all people so that by all possible means I might save some. I do all this for the sake of the gospel, that I may share in its blessings."

The Apostle Paul spiritedly attempted to become all things to all people to win as many people as possible for the Kingdom of God. Paul was apprehended by God. He did not pursue a self-chosen career. Instead, he was given something to steward that he did not seek. His was chosen and sent by God to plant churches and share the gospel with the Gentiles. As a result, Paul had to learn to meet people right where they were. I too have learned, by the grace of God, the value of meeting people right where they are. Now I find myself in this position that I did not seek or pursue, an additional ministry, a calling, something additional to steward. Since losing my son Michael in 2019, God has placed **83 families??? people??? parents???** in front of me who have lost a child. Each of them has had distinctly different circumstances and needs surrounding their loss. If I would have been the least bit insensitive to their unique circumstances, I don't think I would have been chosen for this honor. This new ministry is now part of my journey.

It is vitally important that we all learn to *lessen* our forwardness toward people and become more attuned to meeting their individual needs. Instead of giving the outpouring we want them to have, we should be more concerned with determining their needs and then meeting them. One evening not long ago, I received a phone call from a man that I had not spoken to in almost two and a half years. I met him along the journey to 83, a number that continues to increase. This man had many questions for which he needed answers. Most of those questions pertained to his inability to get back in the flow of life after losing his son. As I do with many of the people who I encounter in this circumstance, I encouraged him. I reminded him that his life had been apprehended by pain and grief and that he didn't need to be so hard on himself.

We spoke about the need to join groups. I reminded him that he needed to be with people who have lived in his circumstances because they could be the ones who not only understood his pain but could bring about real healing. I told him not to forget to press into God because He is the One who has experienced the greatest pain of all and can identify with us in ours.

> *Isaiah 53:3-6 (NIV), "He was despised and rejected by mankind, a man of suffering, and familiar with pain. Like one from whom people hide their faces he was despised, and we held him in low esteem. Surely he took up our pain and bore our suffering, yet we considered him punished by God, stricken by him, and afflicted. But he was pierced for our transgressions, he was crushed for our iniquities; the punishment that brought us peace was on him, and by his wounds we are healed. We all, like sheep, have gone astray, each of us has turned to our own way; and the Lord has laid on him the iniquity of us all."*

He replied, "I have done this, and I have done that. I have done everything! I have prayed. I have asked God for help. I went to a group a few times. I have attended church a few times. I have tried to get on with my life. Everything reminds me that my son is gone. I don't think the things you are suggesting are going to help because I have done them. The pain still haunts me. The grief is still with me. I just want to know when all of this will be over."

I replied, "Congratulations! You are human. You have been afflicted in the worst manner, and you need time to heal. I am twice as far along this journey as you are, and I still have moments of uncertainty and pain that cause me to weep and wail. You need time more than anything else. But time only dulls the pain. Your pain will never leave you, but it will change from a piercing, stabbing, thrusting, knife-like cutting in your chest to a throbbing, numbing, almost debilitating vacant ache. Let me warn you now, although your pain will subside in time, make no mistake it will remain a constant reminder. Life will always be different; it will never be the same. But God will demonstrate His majesty in your circumstances. He will show Himself faithful. Please remember that you are still in the beginning stages of this journey to healing. **I can tell you that God is in your circumstances. He is with you!**"

"How do you know that God is in my circumstances?" the man asked.

"How do I know that God is in your circumstances? Is that your question?", I inquired. I asked yet another question, "What prompted you to call me today?"

The Twelve Most Important Words

He said, "I don't know."

I told him, "You called me because God prompted you to do so. Do you know who else God prompted to contact me today? Earlier today, my deceased son's girlfriend's sister reached out to me via Facebook Messenger. I have never spoken to this person a day in my life. In fact, I didn't even know his girlfriend had a sister. She said that she was cleaning her basement and found my son's basketball and his soccer jersey and thought that I should have possession of them. Tomorrow, I am meeting her to pick up those items. Now let me ask you something. What are the odds that God prompted two people to contact me today? Not just to contact me, but to do it in a specific order. And why did God make all this happen? Because He knew that you were losing hope. He knew that I needed something to share with you to prove that He is in your circumstances. I am here to tell you that God has never left you and He will never leave you."

> *Deuteronomy 31:8 (NIV), "The Lord himself goes before you and will be with you; he will never leave you nor forsake you. Do not be afraid; do not be discouraged."*

At that moment, the man started to cry, and I found myself crying alongside him. He said, "I was wrong Jeff. I was wrong. I called you because I know you know what I am going through. I know God is in my circumstances. Thank you for taking my call. Thank you for showing me hope. Thank you for showing me compassion. Thank you for doing what you do. Thank you for being obedient to God."

I responded, "You are more than welcome. But this phone call was just as much for me as it was for you. Thank you for responding to God's prompting. Remember, God is still with you."

-Scratching old scars-

> *1 Peter 3:8 (NIV), "Finally, all of you, be like-minded, be sympathetic, love one another, be compassionate and humble."*

In my dysfunctional family, there have been a few moments when it appeared we might get past all the division, and for the first time become one family united instead of two broken un-blended families. One of the most hopeful times came just prior to my son Michael's death. The five of us siblings, my two younger brothers who share the same parents and my two younger sisters who share the same father, began meeting to discuss what was important and how we might make unity real. I was so thankful that our coming together was organic and not the result of Michael's death which was just a few months into the unforeseen future. This meant that our unity had a real chance of survival because it wasn't predicated on an event but was natural. However, before our first meeting with all five siblings, I needed to nudge my youngest brother to open his heart. He had closed that chapter of his life and didn't want to revisit it again. He felt very strongly that there was no hope because he had been crushed one too many times, and he didn't want to scratch his old scars.

James is my youngest brother. He was two years old when our parents divorced. As a result, he doesn't have a memory that is "normal." In fact, everything about his life is dysfunctional, and he carries around pain and hurt that he doesn't know how to let go of. When we began having conversations about coming together as five siblings, James was obstinate. He and I had many conversations about what could be and how the right thing, dare I say the best thing, was for all of us to let down our guard. It took many attempts before I was able to convince James to attend a meeting with all his siblings. I grimace at my use of the word convince, which looking back isn't necessarily a good word. After reflecting on what eventually happened at our initial meeting of the five, I realized that not only did I convince James to do something that he didn't want to do, but that he had also made a prediction that was prophetic. James had closed the door of his heart for a reason. He knew what was going to happen.

During our initial meeting, all five siblings agreed to unity *at all costs*. Somehow James knew something the rest of us didn't know. It was then that James said something to our sisters that I will never forget. He looked at them and said, "I feel sorry for you girls. Jeff, Bob, and I have been made to make constant adjustments and compromises, to accept things we didn't want, to learn and grow in ways that we weren't supposed to, but we had to anyway. We have been conditioned by circumstances that we never created. You, on the other hand, have been living in a different world. That is not your fault. But the decisions in front of you will be more challenging than you could possibly imagine. You may have to walk in defiance of your parents for the benefit of this group. Choices that we have been facing for decades, you will face for the first time. I don't think you know what you are entering into with this agreement."

Both girls said they were ready and willing. We all left that meeting with great hope. And at first, things went well. Unfortunately, when the first impossible choice presented itself, unity was not the outcome. Our sisters chose what was familiar to them and proved they weren't ready to make hard choices. Everything quickly crashed from that moment on, and any hope of reconciliation had vanished. That is when we could clearly see the wise words that James had shared during our initial meeting. But that meant that James had allowed his brother, *me*, to manipulate him by exposing himself to greater discomfort and rejection. It was then that I knew that I needed to make amends with him. I had asked my brother, who hadn't known a day of normal in his whole life to trust me. I convinced him that I knew better than him. I wasn't thinking about what he needed, I was more concerned about what I was trying to give him. As a result, I was not loving him at all. I was deeply saddened about what I had done to him and what I had put him through. I called him and said, "James, I was wrong." Thankfully, my brother forgave me.

-Something must change-

Many say that their children are their greatest source of joy, but I think many would agree that they can also be our greatest source of frustration and can show us just how much patience and self-control we may not have, but need by the boatload. In one of those moments of lacking patience and self-control, have you ever lost the last bit of control you had and screamed at one of your children? On this particular day, not only did I lose control, but I also placed myself in my bed for five days with a pulled muscle in my chest. I was coming to grips with the fact that whatever influence I may have had with my son Michael, it was quickly vanishing because I was trying to control him. I knew that if I didn't do something different, I would lose him forever. So, while I was healing from my irresponsible and unhelpful outburst, I decided that I was not going to wait for something to change, *I* was going to change because Michael deserved better.

> *Isaiah 43:19 (NIV), "See, I am doing a new thing! Now it springs up; do you not perceive it? I am making a way in the wilderness and streams in the wasteland."*

My son was out in the world, and he didn't think home was a safe harbor any longer. How was I going to get his attention? How would I gain another chance to prove that Michael was valuable to me? How would I ever persuade him to believe that I was for him and not against him? All these questions could have paralyzed me with fear and caused me not to take action, but by the grace of God, they didn't. I reached out to Michael and asked him if we could have breakfast or lunch sometime. He didn't respond immediately, but eventually he agreed to breakfast. When we sat down to eat, gratitude overwhelmed me to tears. I was grateful for no other reason than to just be able to look at him. My son, who I screamed at with complete terror, was willing to give me another chance.

Michael ordered food that day, but it was clear that he didn't plan to eat. I asked him questions to open our dialogue, but his lack of communication was evidence that my approach wasn't getting us anywhere. That's when I said to Michael, "Son, what happened between us the last time we were together was so wrong. I was wrong. I don't care what you did or didn't do, you did not deserve to be treated that way. The words that came out of my mouth, I wish I could take them back. I know they hurt you. I can't even remember all that I said. I just know it was wrong. All of it. I know that for us to have a relationship, I will need to respect you. I may not like the way you are living your life, but I can respect you. Michael, with every ounce of love that I can gather, I want you to know that I was wrong. I am so sorry. I hope you will be able to forgive me someday. Michael, I love you!"

I am not sure if our relationship would have ever developed into something more meaningful had I not said those words that were on my heart that day at the restaurant. When I look back, remembering the countless men who have sat in my office in despair over their broken relationships with their own children, and thinking about my own tumultuous relationship with my father, I am so grateful for the hand of God on my life. None of this would be possible without Him. When we left the restaurant that day, Michael hugged me as he had always done before. He told me he loved me. I asked if we could have another meal together sometime soon. Thankfully, he agreed.

The Twelve Most Important Words

Jeff Frick

(Sketch by Steve Perucca)

1 Corinthians 13:11 (NIV)
"When I was a child, I talked like a child, I thought like a child, I reasoned like a child. When I became a man, I put the ways of childhood behind me."

3

I Am Sorry

> "Oh, it seems to me that sorry seems to be the hardest word."
> -Elton John

Music can sometimes share things that ordinary spoken words cannot. Songwriters have a true gift that allows them to string together words and melodies that produce songs that evoke emotions, paint vivid pictures, and take us to places we couldn't otherwise travel. Have you ever purchased a blank card to give to someone because you wanted to come up with the most perfect personal message for the recipient, only to have the blank open space inside the card mock you for thinking you could come up with something better to say than the poets at Hallmark? If this has ever been you, I urge you to listen to a few songs pertaining to the message you want to convey in your card to help get your creative juices flowing. Oh, and use a pencil for easy editing as your words meet the paper.

One such song that puts you right on the rollercoaster of emotional turmoil is "Just Say I'm Sorry" sung by Pink and Chris Stapleton, written by Alicia Moore & Chris Stapleton. If you have never listened to this song, I implore you to search for it on your favorite listening venue and give it a listen. The three minute and 34 second rollercoaster of emotion is highlighted by the fact that the song is stripped down to two voices and a guitar that grips you the second the song starts before a voice ever begins to sing. It will speak a message to you that is so clear, I guarantee you will meditate about your relationships and wonder if you have treated well, those that you claim to love. The lyrics of this song are universal to any kind of relationship that imperfect people engage in whether friendships, parent-child, siblings, family, teacher-student, or marriage. If there is an opportunity for you to hurt the opposing party, these lyrics apply. I encourage you to listen to the song all the way through a couple of times. As you listen, let the artist's voice be replaced with the voice of your hurt loved one. Do you need to just say you're sorry?

<u>Just say I'm sorry</u>
Just say I'm sorry
It's not the hardest thing to do
Just say you're wrong sometimes
And I'd believe you; 'Cause I love you
Just say I'm sorry

Everybody wants to be; The one who's right
Everybody wants the last word; To end the fight
Every day is a new day; With a chance to choose
Sometimes the way you win; Is to say you lose
Just say I'm sorry

It's not the hardest thing to do
Just say you're wrong sometimes
And I'd believe you; 'Cause I love you
Just say I'm sorry

Love is a gamble; And the stakes are high
And all that's on the table; Is a bad goodbye
You say you'd die for me; So I don't know why
You can't pull the trigger; And kill your pride
Just say I'm sorry

It's not the hardest thing to do
Just say you're wrong sometimes
And I'd believe you; 'Cause I love you
Just say I'm sorry

It's not the hardest thing to do
Just say you're wrong sometimes
And I'd believe you; 'Cause I love you
Just say I'm sorry, 'Cause I love you

There are many universal truths found in this song that capture every human heart. Let's take a closer look at some of the lyrics that are so perfectly crafted into short little vulnerable phrases that pack a punch and can stop you in your tracks. This song is so powerful that it can bring specific situations into the listener's mind and make them wonder if this song was written specifically about them. Some listeners may be thinking, "Exactly! It's not that hard to just say I'm sorry. What are you waiting for?" While others may listen and feel tortured thinking, "I can't kill my pride because either I wasn't wrong or I don't know how to say that I was, in fact, wrong." Either way, this song surely evokes an emotional response.

First- "Everybody wants to be the one who's right." I had a good friend, Jerry McCloud, who is no longer with us. Jerry used to say, "You can *'right'* yourself right out of a relationship." How much will being *right* cost you? Are you willing to pay the cost of being *right*?

Second- "Everybody wants that last word to end the fight." We somehow believe that if we don't get the last word, we lost the fight. Our desire is to win so we don't lose. We will do anything to ensure we don't lose. When we get the last word, we are proud of ourselves, like we accomplished something of great value. But the only thing we may have accomplished is having one less relationship to keep score of. How sad is that? When the relationship battlefield is so littered with the carnage of a relationship that once was, when will we begin to see that much of the debris was actually caused by friendly fire?

Third- "Every day is a new day with a chance to choose." We all get to choose what we say, when we say it, how we say it, and who we say it to. Sometimes no response is the best response. Have you ever heard of the saying, "less is more?" This phrase can be applied to more than just home decor and fancy plating at a top-notch restaurant. We all have the choice to keep the words that don't serve a purpose but to further destroy our relationships, to ourselves. Oftentimes the less is more option carries the greater value. Both in our relationships and in home furnishings.

Fourth- "Sometimes the way you win is to say you lose." Are we living as though others are more important than ourselves? Or is "me" more important than "we?" The friend I talked about earlier in Chapter One wears one of those silicone bracelets with the saying, "I am Second." Being second is contrary to our culture, but taking the back seat during the storm in a relationship sometimes speaks louder than any point you could try to make or any insult you could hurl in your loved one's direction. Take the "I am Second" approach and watch "I" become "we" as your relationship weathers the storm meant to destroy it. Power resides in your humbleness.

Fifth- "Love is a gamble, and the stakes are high." Aren't the stakes of every relationship high? We won't maintain our relationships if we don't learn how to express our love to the people we claim to value. For those of you reading that are married, let's talk about expressing your love for the person you value. For the person you place above all others, even your children, which I learned all those years ago. Go back and read your wedding vows. Are you living up to the vows you expressed on what I can assume was one of the best days of your life? Do you still hold your spouse in the same high regard now as you did then? Do you live as though the stakes are high and that every day is a chance to show your loved one your commitment? Cherish, forevermore, love, till death do us part, in good times and in bad, promise, commit, before God-these are all fairly common wedding vow buzz words that all sound authentic and high stakes to me. Even if you aren't married, it's safe to bet that you, too, have relationships where the stakes are high and that you too need to recommit to regular maintenance of that relationship. Don't wait until your relationship's 'Check Engine' light comes on to give it the attention it needs. Many times, regular maintenance ensures the relationship 'Check Engine' light doesn't come on or is easily fixed if it does.

Sixth- "And all that's on the table is a bad goodbye." How many relationships have been ruined over one fight, or one fight too many, where someone walked out angry without feeling seen or heard and without their needs being met? Grudges and resentment form when we hold onto anger. Anger doesn't solve anything. It builds nothing, but it can destroy everything.

Seventh- "You say you'd die for me, so I don't know why you can't pull the trigger and kill your pride." This one is all about our identity. "Killing our pride" for some people is a literal killing of themselves. That's because their addiction to control outweighs the humility they haven't yet learned to exercise freely; so, then they would rather *die* than be *wrong*. Jesus calls us to die to self and follow his example. If we don't, our words "***I am sorry***" will always be empty to its recipients.

> *Galatians 2:20 (NIV), "I have been crucified with Christ and I no longer live, but Christ lives in me. The life I now live in the body, I live by faith in the Son of God, who loved me and gave himself for me."*

-First funeral-

Have you ever had a moment of reflection; where you saw something in hindsight that gave you pause? When the moment originally occurred, you weren't sure why it was presented to you. Most human beings are not wired to enter places where they fear what will happen next, especially if it pertains to something they have never experienced previously. However, if we are going to walk with Jesus in an intentional way, our faith must grow to be able to withstand whatever fear we may be feeling. Jesus wants to show us so many wonderful things, but it requires us to trust Him even in the fear.

> *John 14:27 (NIV), "Peace I leave with you; my peace I give you. I do not give to you as the world gives. Do not let your hearts be troubled and do not be afraid."*

I remember one such moment I had many years ago. I was newly trained as a Chaplain but had yet to perform a funeral service. I didn't know when but knew funeral services would be one of the many duties I would be required to carry out. Most new Chaplains believe that they will just be ready when the *moment* arrives. Unfortunately, that just isn't true. Just like with many things we do for the first time, terror gripping fear creeps in and we begin to feel paralyzed by our fear and sometimes don't follow through with what needs to be done or is expected of us. Without follow through, all we are left with are our good intentions that lack appropriate action. This is exactly what happened to me the first time I was asked to perform a funeral.

Maybe it wasn't the funeral itself that brought about my fear. The more I think about it, I have to believe it was probably the fact that the funeral was for a child. I remember the absolute terror that came over me when I was asked to preside over this child's funeral. I responded with, "Maybe you could ask 'so and so?' If not 'so-and-so,' perhaps you could ask 'what's-his-name?' If not 'what's-his-name,' perhaps you could ask 'what's-her-name?' If not 'what's-her-name,' perhaps you could ask 'that guy?' If not 'that guy,' perhaps you could ask 'that person?' If not 'that person,' perhaps you could ask 'a certain someone?' If not a 'certain someone,' perhaps you could ask 'a fellow?' If not 'a fellow,' perhaps you could ask 'a chap?' If not 'a chap,' perhaps you could ask 'a certain party?' If not 'a certain party,' perhaps you could ask 'the aforementioned?' If not 'the aforementioned,' perhaps you could ask simply 'someone?' If not 'someone,' perhaps you could ask 'anyone?' But I need you to ask all those people and maybe even more before you come back to ask me again. At that point, if you still can't find a willing soul, I guess I will be the unwilling one."

As you can tell from my long-winded, time-consuming reply, I had no desire to perform a child's funeral, especially not as my first experience. The fear simply overwhelmed me. I was not ready to walk in obedience to God, the calling He had apparently placed on my life, nor was I ready to bring His comfort to those He had placed in front of me. I thought I was ready, but clearly I was not. Years later, God revealed to me why He was attempting to prepare me for funerals, especially children's funerals. As I began to become more comfortable presiding over funerals of various kinds, I was asked to preside over my cousin's funeral. I had to sit with my aunt and uncle as they stared into space, almost numb, not knowing how to process their loss. But it wasn't until my son Michael died that I was struck on the head with what God had been trying to show me all along.

I remember coming to that realization and crying out to God with a flood of emotions. I remember telling Him how sorry I was for not seeing what He had been trying to show me. I apologized to Him for not walking in obedience. "I am sorry God. I am so sorry," I wept. All along God was with me preparing a way for me because He knows the end even at the beginning. He is the One Who created us. He is the One Who will see His plans through. God is always trying to talk to us, reveal things in us, and is always pursuing us. Do we see and hear Him? We must not because if we did, why would we run in the opposite direction in fear? I am so grateful we can apologize to our Heavenly Father and know that "it is finished." I have learned to appreciate the call that God has placed on my life. Although, if I am being honest, it would not be something that I would choose. However, Father God created me to serve Him in this way to bring glory to His Name.

> *Isaiah 46:9-11 (NIV), "Remember the former things, those of long ago; I am God, and there is no other; I am God, and there is none like me. I make known the end from the beginning, from ancient times, what is still to come. I say, 'My purpose will stand, and I will do all that I please.' From the east I summon a bird of prey; from a far-off land, a man to fulfill my purpose. What I have said, that I will bring about; what I have planned, that I will do."*

Over the next few years, I would preside over a great number of children's funerals and sit with more parents who stared numbly into space so grieved they did not know how to take the next breath. When God calls, you may not like what He has to say, or what He wants to show you. Sometimes, it may be a glimpse into the future that He has for you. The future He has for you may not align with the future you envisioned for yourself. Remember one thing: He is God, and we are not. When you find yourself not walking in obedience to the things He has planned for you, just simply say *"I am sorry"* and know that Jesus has paid the cost. If we are unwilling to say, "I am sorry" to God, who will we share this sentiment with?

-Operator error-

Have you ever experienced a moment in life when you were embarrassed by your own pride and ego? A moment when you thought for sure you were right, and you held your ground only to be proven wrong? Even in our embarrassment, we are to provide a solid apology for our wrongdoing. The following story ended with a heartfelt *"I am sorry"* because I was caught up in my own ego. I cost others a lot of time and money and unnecessarily cost myself much grief.

> Proverbs 12:15 (NIV), "The way of fools seems right to them, but the wise listen to advice."

It was the Fall season. At my house, that means picking up the fallen leaves, I mean a lot of leaves. My normal practice is to get on my riding lawn mower and pick up the leaves like I am cutting grass. This allows the leaves to be broken down and then collected into the attached bags on my lawn mower. Each week as the leaves begin to fall, I fill both of my yard-waste bins with leaves and set them out on trash day for pick up. By doing so, I maintain the leaves as they fall each week, which prevents me from having to manually rake and bag them. Which by the way is my least favorite way to pick up leaves. A week or two into the Fall season this year, my mower broke down and it was necessary for me to call the local repair shop and make arrangements for them to pick up my mower to fix whatever had caused it to break down. My mower was picked up three days later.

A few days after the pick-up, I was informed by the repair shop that my riding lawn mower needed a new carburetor. Upon completion of the repair, I had to schedule for the mower to be dropped off to ensure someone would be home to receive it. Three days later, the delivery man started my mower to get it off the truck and parked it in my garage. I had no need to use it that evening, so I left it there until I could find a window of opportunity to pick up the leaves which were now piling up. The next day my grandson was visiting and wanted to get some of his toys out so he could play. This required me to move the lawn mower. I tried to start it, but it would not turn over. I thought, "How could it start yesterday and not start today?" Aggravated, I called the repair shop and informed them that the repair that was done was incomplete. I scheduled yet another time for the pick-up and servicing of my mower. It was picked up three days later.

After spending a day troubleshooting my no-start mower, the repair shop informed me of their findings. The repair order stated that the mower was started, used to cut some grass, then was left to run for two hours, and then finally the gas was replaced. In the end, the repair shop said they were unable to duplicate my problem, and no additional charges were incurred. I now had to schedule yet another drop-off of my mower back to my home. At this point, it had become necessary for me to rake and bag my leaves the hard way and I wasn't pleased. Three days later, my mower arrived, and the driver once again started the mower to remove it from his truck and parked it in my garage. About an hour later, I tried to start the mower and once again it would not start.

At this point I was getting very frustrated that I would have to go through the process of waiting for another pick up day so the repairmen could diagnose the problem. In addition, I was leaving in two days to go out of town for a convention. So, I decided to take a video of the mower not starting, hoping this would help the repair shop quickly find a solution to the problem. I called the shop and sent the video, and the operator told me that a manager would be calling me the next morning. I was going to be traveling by the shop later that day before they closed, and for a brief moment, I thought about walking in and raising the temperature just a little. I wanted them to know that I was not pleased and if they could forgo their normal practice of a three-day pick-up and drop-offs, especially when *they* had caused me additional aggravation because the repair was incomplete. However, I decided that was probably not the best way to handle this situation.

By 11a.m. the next day, I had not heard from the manager, so I decided to take another video of the mower not starting. I sent this video to the repair shop as well. About an hour later, I received a call from the manager. He indicated that he would be coming by my house in 10 minutes to take a look at the mower and verified that I would be home.

Upon arriving, he asked me when I had last tried to start the mower. I told him that I had tried just this morning and yet again had not been able to get it to start. He asked me to show him what I was doing when trying to start the mower. So, I attempted to start it while he watched, and yet again it would not start. That's when the manager said, "That's what I thought." He reached for the throttle lever and placed it in the choke position, then said to try it again. Instantly it started. He placed the throttle back in the normal position and then smirked. I believe he was trying with all his might to not be mean to me or embarrass me any further.

I looked at him and said, "I am so sorry! I am sorry for causing all the unnecessary excitement. All the running back and forth and the time spent looking at a problem that was never a problem at all."

The manager said, "It's quite all right. These things happen."

I thought for a moment and told him that I have owned this mower for more than two years and have never used the choke. After telling him it has always eventually started without using the choke, he informed me that with a new carburetor and the falling temperatures, the throttle will always need to be in the choke position for the mower to start. I promised to get into the habit of putting the throttle in the choke position so as to prevent my mower from needing servicing in the future when the temperatures begin to fall. He asked if he could do anything else to help and then left after I thanked him. I sat there for a few minutes thinking, "All of this has been the result of embarrassing *operator error*. I was so sure that they had done something wrong and that I had been the one who was mistreated. I could have saved myself a lot of grief and aggravation. How could I be so stupid?"

> *Luke 14:11 (NIV), "For all those who exalt themselves will be humbled, and those who humble themselves will be exalted."*

-On someone else's behalf-

How many times have you been somewhere with someone and they say or do something that you feel is so egregious that it warrants an "I am sorry" from you because it was never said by the person who said or did whatever you felt was out of line? I would be willing to bet that you can name quite a few instances. The real question is, did you actually say

"*I am sorry*" on the other person's behalf or did you let it go hoping that the recipient didn't take too much offense to it? Whether you did or didn't, did you at least question the person you were with and ask them why they were so harsh and inconsiderate? Sometimes, it is necessary to confront our friends and family to remind them that we should always be respectful of others and that not everything should elicit a response from us when we feel slighted.

After writing and publishing my first book, "How do I Love my *Neighbor*? 4 PROMISES AND 6 TRUTHS" my friend Bob, a pastor from Pennsylvania suggested that we go on a book signing tour to promote my book. I had never considered a promotional tour, but it sounded exciting and would be something fun to do with my friend. Bob made all the arrangements and scheduled all the places we would be visiting in the northeastern United States to promote my book. I didn't give much thought to the places we would be going, nor where we would be staying, but I trusted Bob and his plethora of contacts to take care of the details.

The tour was scheduled to start before the books would have been shipped to my house in Michigan, so I made arrangements for them to be delivered to another printing building in Pennsylvania that is owned by my publisher. As it turned out, even with the new shipping arrangements, the books were still delayed by a couple of days. In that couple of days, I found myself almost to the point of anger towards Bob because of his harsh and callous language. I couldn't believe that someone could treat people with such disregard, especially being a pastor.

While waiting for the books, we visited a 24-hour prayer church. There we met a young Amish man named Seth. During our conversation, Seth invited us to his house to meet his family. It wasn't long before we were in Lancaster County, Pennsylvania, which is probably one of the largest and oldest Amish communities. We visited with Seth's family for a few hours and began thinking about where we would be heading next because we were still waiting for books to be delivered. That's when Seth invited us to attend his Friday night Bible study with about 15 of his friends.

We entered the home where the Bible study was held and were introduced to all the men. Barely five minutes into our visit, while conversing about what they were studying, Bob found himself in a verbal altercation with one of the young men we had just met. Bob wouldn't give an inch in his verbal assault and was arguing over what many would consider very trivial things. Finally, Bob found himself in a place with nowhere to go. He painted himself into a corner, so to speak, and couldn't get out. His antics were dreadful. That's when he looked at me and almost screamed, "Aren't you going to do something? Are you just going to leave me here?"

I looked at Bob and said, "You want me to untie these strings? Okay Bob! Sure!"

Proverbs 21:23 (NIV), "Those who guard their mouths and their tongues keep themselves from calamity."

I turned to the group and said, "I am sorry, gentlemen. It appears that my friend Bob is acting out of sorts. You have been very kind to invite us to participate in your Bible study and I am very sorry for my friend's behavior. I am sure he won't bring any more trouble to your home."

When the Bible study was over, Seth said to Bob and me, "It's very late. I just realized that you haven't secured a place to stay for the evening." He looked over at one of the other men and said, "Jason, you have spare rooms, I need you to put these men up for the night." At this, Jason called his wife and told her to prepare the spare rooms because he was bringing men home with him who needed a place to stay.

When we arrived at Jason's home, it was very dark and hard to see anything outside. We had to follow him closely. When we entered the living room, we found Jason's wife wearing her traditional long sleeve dress with a full skirt, apron and bonnet. She greeted us in a way that I don't think I have ever been greeted before. She was so excited that we would be staying in her home. She said that they enjoy being hospitable and then she gave us the lay of the land. She said, "I have changed the sheets on the beds. You will find your rooms upstairs to the right. On the left side of the hallway is a prayer room. Feel free to use the prayer room as frequently and as long as you like. Our house is old, but we have converted a wonderful bathroom in the basement for all to enjoy. There you will find towels, soap, and shampoo. If there is anything else that you need, please let me know. Again, it is our greatest honor to have you stay with us."

That's when Bob chimed in saying, "All that sounds great, but I want to know what time you are serving us breakfast?"

The woman didn't bat an eye and said, "7:30 sharp."

I was so angry I could have punched Bob in the throat. But instead, I apologized profusely to the kind woman for my friend's poor conduct. At that, we all went to bed.

> *Ephesians 4:29 (NIV), "Do not let any unwholesome talk come out of your mouths, but only what is helpful for building others up according to their needs, that it may benefit those who listen."*

The next morning, we had a fabulous breakfast unlike anything I had ever eaten or seen. We also got a chance to walk around the grounds of their property. The house was built in the 1800's and was very beautiful. Jason and his wife were headed to a fair in town and asked if we would like to come. Bob was quick to say yes. This couple paid our entry fees and bought us drinks and snacks all while insisting that we were to receive their hospitality. When we returned to their home later that day, Bob pushed the yardstick from an inch to a mile and said that we should be guests in their home for another night. He seemed to guilt the couple into agreeing. Again, I felt uncomfortable. I apologized once again for my friend's forwardness and thanked them for their kindness.

The next morning, we were off to upstate New York to visit one of Bob's friends. We drove most of the day to get there. During our drive, Bob didn't fill me in on what we would be walking into, I just followed him in. This house was a mansion built in the early 1900's. It needed some work like most old homes do, but it was beautiful. How many homes built in the early 1900's have walk-in closets in the bedrooms? Not just the primary bedrooms, but every bedroom?

When we walked into the kitchen, Bob said, "Good evening, Angie! What have you prepared for us for dinner?" Angie hadn't started cooking anything yet, but did say she was going to be making spaghetti soon. I thought it was odd that Angie was home alone and that her husband was never mentioned. I wondered why we would be staying in this woman's house if she was single. Is that appropriate? But Bob set all our plans, so I trusted him.

After dinner we got better acquainted. Sitting in her kitchen, she began to tell me her story. Angie broke down and started to cry explaining that her husband had died only six weeks earlier. Clearly, she was in the sharp pain of early grief. She said, "My husband did all our banking. He was the one who had all our passwords. I have no access to money. I can't even get into the safe in my bedroom."

This was heartbreaking news that would have been nice to know before we walked into her home. Again, I began to get angry at Bob. He knew all these important details and instead of asking how Angie was doing, or if there was anything we could do to help, Bob demanded dinner be prepared. I apologized to her saying, "Angie, I am so sorry for your loss. I am sorry for how Bob spoke to you. I am sorry that I didn't know your circumstances before we arrived. I would have said something to Bob had I known. I will be praying for your healing and financial circumstances to change." I spent the next four hours ministering to this woman who desperately needed someone to listen and care.

> *Proverbs 15:4 (NIV), "The soothing tongue is a tree of life, but a perverse tongue crushes the spirit."*

Bob is a very unique fellow. To be fair, his friends know him for who he is and expect nothing less from him. Also, the people we met in Lancaster County are genuinely friendly and accepting, wanting to provide hospitality in any way they can. Bob knows this because he has spent his whole life in that area of the country. But beneath Bob's gruff exterior and lack of basic manners, he loves Jesus. I have witnessed the Holy Spirit use him in amazing ways. Bob has a church that I was invited to preach at and was the guest of honor during a luncheon that followed. I don't say all this to give Bob a pass. Like we all do, he surely needs to tighten up his words. Because of this, when I am with him, I find myself saying "*I am sorry*" on his behalf many times and in many different situations.

-Never have I said-

Let me ask a serious question. How can a single person get through life without the words "*I am sorry*" ever escaping their lips? Have you ever met a person who fits this description? It's hard to believe that there are people who have lived for any length of time and have not shared those words. It's puzzling, but these people do exist. Maybe you have met one along the way? I know that I have met my fair share of the not so sorry crowd. I actually know a man who is almost *proud* of the fact that he has never uttered the words, "***I am sorry.***"

I met this man when he was referred by a mutual friend to come and sit with me. This friend said that I could probably help him sort some things out in his life. We met many times and each time he felt more comfortable to share elements of his life from the past that he hoped would have turned out differently. He had been married and divorced twice before but desperately wants a connection with someone. His longing to be in a relationship with someone is part of our human existence on this planet and is a part of the journey of life as God created us to be in relationship, in community, to be connected.

> *Ecclesiastes 4:9-12 (NIV), "Two are better than one, because they have a good return for their labor: If either of them falls down, one can help the other up. But pity anyone who falls and has no one to help them up. Also, if two lie down together, they will keep warm. But how can one keep warm alone? Though one may be overpowered, two can defend themselves. A cord of three strands is not quickly broken."*

Each time we met, he would share some of his adventures in dating. However, he could never seem to find anyone who suited him. They were either too heavy, or too short, or didn't have the right job, or didn't bring anything to the relationship in terms of material possessions. As we would talk in depth about his desire for the *perfect* person, it became clear to me that he was lacking in the understanding of what love truly is. I asked him many times to consider the elements that are necessary for love to exist. Love cannot exist without *our* sacrifice and *their* free will. I asked him what would happen if he met his *perfect* person? What would happen over time, through the natural process of aging, if she gained a few pounds or developed a few wrinkles? Would he then leave her? Would her exterior characteristics then outweigh all the things he loved about her that aren't outwardly visible? Everyone has quirks that make them unique. You have them, I have them. When those quirks become endearing, we know that we have learned to love a person well. Are you searching for the *perfect* person, so you don't have to love anyone but yourself? Those types of questions seemed to bother him immensely.

As we dug deeper into his previous experiences in marriage, he shared with me all the things that he used to do and say that he now realized were unkind. He shared how he treated his previous wives with disrespect and had a lack of concern for their needs. He wanted his needs met, but didn't care about trying to meet their needs. Basically, his relationships were not loving relationships, they were one-sided and lacked any kind of depth you'd expect in a healthy marriage. His lack of concern and complete disregard for their needs conveyed a nasty message he didn't even have to verbally speak, "I don't want to be an active participant in this marriage, so therefore I will be doing the bare minimum and will not be shouldering any of the difficult *heavy lifting* that is required in a marriage. If you don't want to shoulder these burdens on your own, I will leave. There's the door if you don't want to comply." When he finally shared that he knew he had made some mistakes, I asked him what he planned to do about it. That's when he said something that I didn't expect to hear.

His response was, "I am not going to do anything about it. I have never said 'I am sorry' a single time in my life."

I was flabbergasted! "You mean to tell me that you have never made a single mistake in your entire life? You have never intentionally or unintentionally harmed a person? You have never said something to a person that you knew you shouldn't have? How is it that you have never shared 'I am sorry' with a single person?" I asked.

His response, "Never have I said I am sorry."

As the weeks went by, this man began to wrestle with God about how to become less selfish and more loving. He seemed to want to make changes in his life and change the way he views people, but he always found a roadblock. That roadblock is himself. As we talked further about his relationship difficulties, which is every person's difficulty because we are all naturally selfish, I reminded him that his problem isn't a "him" problem, it's a human problem. We are all in the same boat. We all need God! He is the place where love begins. Without Him, we are trying to love people from an empty source. He is *the* Source.

> *1 John 4:19-21 (NIV), "We love because he first loved us. Whoever claims to love God yet hates a brother or sister is a liar. For whoever does not love their brother and sister, whom they have seen, cannot love God, whom they have not seen. And he has given us this command: Anyone who loves God must also love their brother and sister."*

This man continues to wrestle with God. However, when he is faced with the difficulties of change and growth, he resists. Again, this is something we all face from time to time. The danger comes when we know we should do something but refuse to do it anyway. In my first book, "How do I Love my *Neighbor*? 4 PROMISES AND 6 TRUTHS" I outline a truth we all grapple with: Once you learn a new truth you cannot unlearn it. We must practice releasing control and comfort by walking with God daily. At times, this man had become so rattled at the thought of changing his ways that he had gone so far as to say, "I have all the God I need. I am satisfied with what I have. I don't need anymore! I don't want anymore!"

The first time I heard him speak those words, I replied, "You have never said 'I am sorry' to anyone. But I think you should consider saying 'I am sorry' to God right now." He and I continue to discuss how to move forward God's way.

It's one thing to say, "I am a work in progress and continue to grow so that I can continue to move forward." It's quite another to say, "I refuse!" We get good at what we practice. We are always practicing something. The question is, "Do we know the difference between growing to make forward progress and refusing to grow and progress?" Growth for moving forward is hard and refusing to grow which leads to no progress at all is hard. Choose your hard.

-One and done-

How many of us have never heard the words "*I am sorry*" from those closest to us? I am talking about not hearing those words from our families; from the people we don't choose to have in our lives. More specifically, I am referring to our mothers and fathers. Our parents, the people who have the ability to encourage and inspire us to bigger and better things throughout our lives. Why would they choose not to humble themselves by saying, "*I am sorry,*" especially when we have shared with them our deepest pain caused by their outburst or lack of care toward us? Let's be very clear, it is a *choice* to withhold encouragement and to not speak life into your children and say, "*I am sorry,*" when you have done something wrong. Sadly, my father is one of those parents.

> *Matthew 12:35-37 (NIV), "A good man brings good things out of the good stored up in him, and an evil man brings evil things out of the evil stored up in him. But I*

tell you that everyone will have to give account on the day of judgment for every empty word they have spoken. For by your words you will be acquitted, and by your words you will be condemned."

I have spent more than four decades attempting to understand my father. I have wanted to quit this seemingly elusive endeavor more times than I can count over the years. I have been frustrated, hurt, aggravated, wounded, despaired, and left in complete amazement by my father's behavior. We have shared an on again off again relationship for more than 40 years. If it wasn't for the fact that he is my father, I would have never attempted to understand him or attempted to restore our relationship for this long. This is not a relationship, or lack thereof, that I would endure for anyone else. Sometimes I believe that God allows things to happen to bring about awareness, growth, character, integrity, and long-suffering in us. My father *is* that person in my life. It wouldn't do any good for me to share the countless stories that have shaped our relationship into what it is today. Nor would it do any good for me to try to paint a vivid picture that explains the depth of what is lacking in his life, and consequently in mine.

The best thing for me to do is simply say that as father and son, we are estranged. We are estranged, but it never had to be that way. That isn't the way that I wanted it to be, and in a strange way I don't think my father wanted it that way either. Disappointingly, this is our reality. Our estrangement didn't happen overnight, and it didn't come as a result of a lack of fighting for unity. In fact, I have approached my father hundreds of times hoping that this would be the day that things would be different and that this time he would change, so that we could begin to grow into the relationship that God had intended. I won't tell you that I haven't made mistakes along the way, because I have made many. In fact, more than I can count. What I can honestly share with you is that I have shared these words with my father regularly: "Dad, I am sorry. You didn't deserve that. You deserve better. I am truly sorry."

Over the years, the same estrangement that I have experienced with my father has become the *norm* in my family. He has an estranged relationship with both of my brothers, all of our wives, and all of our children. Over the years, I have heard my brothers say these words to him, "If you could have said, *'I am sorry'* once or twice along the way, maybe things wouldn't be so broken between us." That's why I included the song at the beginning of this chapter. When I first heard it, I believed that song was written about my father's relationship with the majority of his family. The words, "Just say I'm sorry, it's not the hardest thing to do, just say you're wrong sometimes and I'd believe you 'cause I love you," can begin to shift the pain in any room for any person if said meaningfully. Then the song gets to the very heart of every conflict by asking a question about pride. The words, "You say you'd die for me so I don't know why you can't pull the trigger and kill your pride. Just say I'm sorry," speaks to the pride in all of us. Sometimes we all need to pull the trigger and kill the pride that keeps adding a brick to the wall that is mounting between us.

Not long ago, I had asked my father why he has never said I am sorry. He said something that he has said many times before. His response was, "I have done nothing wrong!" I reminded him that people make mistakes all the time and that people harm others unintentionally. If a person says that you have harmed them, and if you claim to love them, why would you not apologize to them?

Then I asked him, "Have you ever made a mistake in your life? Because by your actions and lack of accountability, one would have to assume that you have lived a perfect, sinless life."

It was then that he uttered, "I'm sorry. There! Are you happy now?" They were empty words followed by the same estranged behavior. He was not sorry. But one thing was for sure, I could no longer claim that he didn't say the words, "I am sorry." I will never hear them again as he is wed to his pride before anything else in this life. That phrase was a one and done!

> *Proverbs 27:2 (NIV), "Let someone else praise you, and not your own mouth; an outsider, and not your own lips."*

-A promise made-

I thought about the relationship, or lack thereof, that I have with my father. Was I doomed to repeat the same generational curse with Michael? I had no excuse if I were to let that happen. My father's circumstances were very different from mine. I could not sit with my father and ask the hard questions, attempting to bring about righteousness in our extended family, and then not seek the same for my own household. I am thankful that we have a choice to value people, and that we can make mistakes, apologize, and ask for forgiveness. These are all aspects of strengthening relationships and growing as people. We either get better or we get bitter. We either grow in our love for each other or we grow further apart. My father's words were now ringing in my ear, "Our family is not unlike most, and I'm good with that." He never wanted more, he never wanted to work for better. He took the easy path instead of the road less traveled. I didn't want that for my family. I didn't want to lose my son, trying to save my dad. I needed to exert the same energy making my own house right as I did struggling to help my father mend his.

Now that Michael was willing to meet with me and to continue to build on our relationship, it was time that I made him a promise, a promise that no father should ever have to make to his son. It still turns my stomach to think that I treated my son so badly and acted in a way that was so outrageous that this promise was needed in the first place. However, this was the place where I was standing because of my poor behavior exhibited towards my son. On this day, I looked at Michael and said, "Michael, please hear me. I have treated you poorly in the past, I have yelled, I have screamed, and I have acted inappropriately toward you. From this day forward, I promise never to do those things to you again. Never! ***I am sorry!*** I am so sorry that you had to endure such horrible behavior from any person, but especially your father. I love you, Michael. You deserve better. You will receive better. I make this promise to you today."

> *Ephesians 6:1-4 (NIV), 'Children, obey your parents in the Lord, for this is right. "Honor your father and mother"—which is the first commandment with a promise— "so that it may go well with you and that you may enjoy long life on the earth." Fathers, do not exasperate your children; instead, bring them up in the training and instruction of the Lord.'*

Over the next few years, our relationship blossomed. We communicated more often and spent more time together. That didn't mean that Michael wasn't still caught up in the world. He was. We had to face many challenges. However, we faced them with self-control and respect for each other. Michael would often say to me, "Dad, I like the way that you talk to me." Hearing those words, after treating Michael the way I did, was so joyous.

God has so many things for us to know about Him. All we must do is sit in the attraction of our relationship with Him and He begins to show us there is a reason why we should do things the way He commands us. If we are willing to humble ourselves and stay obedient to His Word, blessings *will* follow. You can't know the depth of Michael's words spoken to me until you have been on the other side. I could have easily destroyed whatever shred of a relationship we had left the night I terrorized my son, but by the grace of God, today was another new day with a new beginning.

> *Jeremiah 29:11 (NIV), "'For I know the plans I have for you," declares the Lord, "plans to prosper you and not to harm you, plans to give you hope and a future."'*

The Twelve Most Important Words

(Sketch by Steve Perucca)

Matthew 6:14-15 (NIV)
"For if you forgive other people when they sin against you, your heavenly Father will also forgive you. But if you do not forgive others their sins, your Father will not forgive your sins."

4

Please Forgive Me

"When we don't forgive, we are bound to our anger, to our anguish, to our pain. We don't recognize that because we feel victorious in our grudge holding. We feel righteous in hanging on to the ways we have been wronged, but forgiving someone does not release accountability. It doesn't mean that you're ok with what happened. Forgiveness means that we accept what happened, we recognize that it can't be undone, and we choose to release the power it has over us."
-Author Unknown

Forgiveness should never rest upon the size of the offense nor the depth of the relationship. Forgiveness should be as easily given as it has been received. If God has forgotten the offense, so should you!

> *Psalm 103:12 (NIV), "as far as the east is from the west, so far has he removed our transgressions from us."*

The problem with forgiveness is that it is not a human trait, it's a supernatural act. Your capacity for self-forgiveness isn't found in you, it's found in Jesus Christ Himself!

> *Luke 23:34 (NIV), 'Jesus said, "Father, forgive them, for they do not know what they are doing." And they divided up his clothes by casting lots.'*

The difficulty we find in forgiveness stems from our ability, or lack thereof, to receive God's forgiveness. Forgiveness is arguably the greatest miracle we experience as human beings because it is truly God's love in action. When we forgive, we extend God's love and release the person who harmed us and at the same time we accept the betrayal just as God has done for us. Throughout our lives, we will often be hurt by others, either intentionally or unintentionally. In the same way, the opposite is true, we will also hurt others, either intentionally or unintentionally. I would make the argument that most people don't wake up in the morning with the intention to harm other people. But, in the heat of the moment, we simply offer the best we have which, all too often results in unintentionally harming others, usually the ones we claim to love. Unfortunately, how we handle that hurt determines our happiness.

Knowing that we will unintentionally harm others throughout life should propel us to seek their forgiveness when we do. Asking for forgiveness is our taking responsibility for and acknowledging that we have harmed someone. It lets the person who we have harmed know that not only are they valuable to us, but that our relationship with them is valuable to us and brings joy to our lives. The actions that follow our appeal will determine if our words were real or simply lip service. If Jesus is Lord of your life, you have no recourse but to practice forgiveness. The lack of forgiveness has caused confusion, division, and poverty in the world. In fact, friendships are dying for lack of forgiveness.

> *Matthew 18:21-22 (NIV), 'Then Peter came to Jesus and asked, "Lord, how many times shall I forgive my brother or sister who sins against me? Up to seven times?" Jesus answered, "I tell you, not seven times, but seventy-seven times."'*

-Houston in Italy-

A couple of years ago, my brother Bob and I decided to take a trip to London to fulfill a desire that he didn't reach in celebrating his 50th birthday a few years prior. As we were planning the trip, we decided that we would attend a concert on the day we arrived in London and another concert on the day before we departed. Thinking that jet lag, flight delays, and any other unforeseen travel difficulties could cause us to arrive in London late, thus missing the concert, we decided to leave a few days earlier than we had initially planned. Had we not arrived as planned, we would have been very disappointed if we had to miss the first concert. With our new schedule arrangements, we would be spending 13 days in London. We were really looking forward to spending some time together across the pond.

A few months before we were to leave, my brother had a thought that we might get bored with so many days in one spot. With this in mind, he made arrangements for us to take a short siesta from London to Italy in the middle of our stay to break things up that offered us even more to see and explore. As it turned out, we could have spent the entire time in

The Twelve Most Important Words

London as it is a very large city with many sites and neighboring countries to explore. But since neither of us had ever been across the pond, we were unaware of all there was to do. As it turned out, the first concert was canceled because of the death of one of the band members, so Italy was the perfect addition.

After checking into our hotel in Italy, we asked the front desk attendant where we could find a good restaurant for dinner. The attendant said that everyone goes down to the beach to enjoy dinner and that we could find many restaurants to choose from in that area. My brother and I made our way down the cliff, nearly a mile walk, and arrived at a wonderful restaurant. We couldn't believe we were enjoying Italy's finest cuisine right on the shore of the Mediterranean Sea. During dinner, we shared some small talk with the table next to us. They were a family of five; mom, dad, and three daughters from Houston, Texas. We couldn't help but think about how it was even possible that we could be sitting next to a family from our own country, as we were not in a touristy part of Italy.

After we ate dinner, we enjoyed dessert and cappuccino. That's when the family at the table next to us asked us to join them at their table. We sat down and shared with each other how it came to be that we were in Italy. The family was enjoying a celebratory dinner because their oldest daughter had just graduated from a university abroad. They were returning home the next morning. After sharing a bit more chit chat about their background, the oldest daughter placed her elbows on the table with interlocked fingers and her chin resting on the back of her hands and asked a question. In a curious and sultry voice, she asked, "So…how did you boys meet?" Both my brother and I started laughing. It was clear to us that this family from Houston; mom, dad, and all three daughters thought we were together, as partners.

I responded by saying, "I met my brother when our mother brought him home from the hospital when I was two years old." The looks on their faces were of complete surprise and embarrassment. It never occurred to them for a moment that we could be brothers.

What happened next was all God. I am not sure why, but maybe because we were not offended and didn't get angry by their assumption, the mother decided to share that she was battling cancer and had just had her last chemo treatment before they left Houston. She pulled off the wig she was wearing to reveal what she had so carefully tried to hide. Each person in the family shared their deepest fears and pains of what lay ahead for their wife and mother. What they didn't know is that my wife had already battled cancer and so had I.

> *2 Corinthians 1:3-5 (NIV), "Praise be to the God and Father of our Lord Jesus Christ, the Father of compassion and the God of all comfort, who comforts us in all our troubles, so that we can comfort those in any trouble with the comfort we ourselves receive from God. For just as we share abundantly in the sufferings of Christ, so also our comfort abounds through Christ."*

I sat there and ministered to each of them for almost two hours while my brother watched and listened. Sadly, they were a family fighting a single battle in three different camps. Mom was on one island, dad was on another, and the three daughters were on yet another. After they bared their souls, obviously living in great fear of the unknown, the mom apologized for her family's assumption by saying, "Please forgive us!"

I replied, "You are already forgiven. Don't give it a second thought. You have much bigger things to worry about. Please take care of yourself and be with your family. We will pray for you."

It was interesting to me that the apology and their asking for forgiveness didn't occur until after they were treated with kindness. I don't know if our kindness was the catalyst for their appeal or not. What I do know is that they experienced God in their most vulnerable moment. They were seen, they were heard, and they were valued. They also wanted us to know that they were thankful, which brought about the apology. On the way back to our hotel, I was trying to imagine all the dots that God had to connect to make our exchange possible. Here we were in a remote part of a foreign country only to find a piece of home right next to us.

My brother asked me, "How were you able to minister to them like that?"

I said, "I didn't. But God did!"

-Horrible husband-

At the time of writing this book, my wife and I have been married for 33 years. Over that span, I have learned many things. The best thing that ever happened to me was receiving

The Twelve Most Important Words

the Lord Jesus Christ as my Savior. When I met my wife, I did not know Jesus. I always believed there was a God, but I didn't know there was a relationship available with Him. Following Jesus has proven to be one of the hardest, and at the same time, most beautiful things I have ever done. Through my journey of faith, Jesus continues to bring revelation knowledge, wisdom, and discernment through a relationship that never ceases to amaze me.

> *Romans 12:1-2 (NIV), "Therefore, I urge you, brothers and sisters, in view of God's mercy, to offer your bodies as a living sacrifice, holy and pleasing to God—this is your true and proper worship. Do not conform to the pattern of this world, but be transformed by the renewing of your mind. Then you will be able to test and approve what God's will is—his good, pleasing and perfect will."*

When my children were young, I did something that many parents fall victim to. I placed my children above my wife. In the Kingdom of God, God illustrates a hierarchy of where our focus should rest. God says, first Him, then your spouse, then your children, then family and finally, your friends. Like many people, I blurred the order of hierarchy. I did this because I was ignorant of my responsibilities as a husband and father because I didn't know the Lord Jesus Christ. Even long-time Christ followers sometimes misconstrue the proper order of hierarchy because we get caught up in our children's lives, activities and their need for our hands-on involvement during different seasons of their development. There are seasons when all our time is spent cheering them on in sporting events, dance recitals and other extracurricular activities. If we don't have a relationship with Jesus, the order that God emphasizes will likely remain skewed in us forever.

The really ugly part of this story is how I treated my wife when I didn't know who Jesus was. I loved my children and placed them higher than anything. So much so, that I would look at my wife and say these words, "Honey, if we were in a boating accident and I could only save three people, you will always be the one who is lost at sea." No matter if she would insist I save our children had this scenario ever been a reality, isn't the point. She probably would have told me to do exactly that, but that doesn't change that I was still wrong in placing our children above her. To make things worse, I would say these words with an almost sinister joy without regard to how my wife might feel upon hearing them. If I can take it one step further, I would even say these words in front of other people. Not because I didn't care about my wife and want what was best for her; but because I was so full of pride for my children. And because I didn't understand the order of hierarchy, I never considered how those words could make her feel because I genuinely believed that my thought process was correct-a little smug but correct. Those words are tough to hear once but hearing them over and over just added insult to injury. And if that wasn't enough, I truly have no idea how many years I peppered my wife with these ugly words. All I know is that I did this to my wife, the person who has stood by me now for 33 years. In going back and rereading these couple paragraphs I even see, what is truly just a grammatical oversight, how I refer to the children. *My* children. Correction, *our* children.

It pains me to know that I did this to the person in which I shared these vows, "For better, for worse, for richer, for poorer, in sickness and in health, to love and to cherish, until parted by death." She was the one who endured the nine uncomfortable months, on three separate occasions, to bring these special people into our lives. She was the one I was disregarding, disrespecting, and treating like yesterday's trash. Can I make it even worse? I think I can. I was oblivious to my actions for many years. After I met Jesus I learned the error in my ways and stopped casting those ugly words in her direction; yet I had never apologized or asked for forgiveness for my blatant disregard for her as my wife. I was oblivious until God's appointed day.

> *1 Corinthians 9:27 (NIV), "No, I strike a blow to my body and make it my slave so that after I have preached to others, I myself will not be disqualified for the prize."*

I have the privilege of sitting with many men to help guide and point them to Jesus. Together, we discover their own works of ministry and uncover their talents and abilities. Oftentimes, while I am in session with someone, I will think about myself as a witness. The thought that always crosses my mind is this: "Does my life reflect the things I am asking this man to do?" One day, a man came to me with marriage problems. He said that he and his wife were living their lives through their children. He said that they didn't know how to communicate with one another. He said that if it wasn't for their children, they would probably get divorced. I told the man that God has a hierarchy and that his wife was to come before his children.

When I heard myself speak those words, I remembered all those years that I treated my wife so poorly. It was then that I finally realized that I had never asked her, or God, for forgiveness regarding my actions and lack of caring. I approached my wife later that night and started a dialogue to discuss my poor behavior from the past and how I had hurt her with my words and actions. I told her that I needed her to know that I was wrong, and that I was sorry. I begged for her to forgive me and told her how much I loved her. She forgave me even after I had continuously spoken words that cut like a knife. Even after all the years that had passed before I apologized, she gave me the gift of forgiveness and grace. Thank you Jesus!

-Talking invites healing-

God continues to place many different people in front of me who have lost children. I am not sure why He chose me to serve Him in this way; however, it is one of the areas of ministry that has been added to my repertoire, probably because of my son, Michael's, passing. I don't get to choose who He puts in my path; my job is just to remain obedient. Sometimes the interactions are a surprise, sometimes they are painful, sometimes they are challenging, but *every* interaction with a parent who has lost a child is just plain *heavy*. The surprise moments occur when it is not immediately evident why I am meeting the person God sent me. Through persistent interaction we always seem to find out why God has joined us together. The challenging times usually occur when I have multiple interactions with people who have lost children.

The multiple interactions aren't as prevalent as the single encounters but can be more agonizing as they always focus on the intense pain, grief, loss of ambition, and the thought that it will never get better. Understandably, the people who I encounter desperately want to know when this season will be behind them. When I receive repeated calls from these people, I usually try to point them in the direction of a group that focuses specifically on dealing with and healing from grief. I do, however, want each of these people to know that they *can* call me *whenever* they want. I do this because there were people available for me when I lost my son, and I want them to have the same opportunity. In addition, God has made it clear that I am to be welcoming to those who are hurting.

Romans 12:3-8 (NIV), "For by the grace given me I say to every one of you: Do not think of yourself more highly than you ought, but rather think of yourself with sober judgment, in accordance with the faith God has distributed to each of you. For just as each of us has one body with many members, and these members do not all have the

> same function, so in Christ we, though many, form one body, and each member belongs to all the others. We have different gifts, according to the grace given to each of us. If your gift is prophesying, then prophesy in accordance with your faith; if it is serving, then serve; if it is teaching, then teach; if it is to encourage, then give encouragement; if it is giving, then give generously; if it is to lead, do it diligently; if it is to show mercy, do it cheerfully."

On one such occasion, I was speaking with a person for the tenth or more times. Like I said, this is quite all right as I want to be available to help in any way that I can. This person was still in the early stages of their loss, and they kept telling me that they didn't feel ready to sit in a group. This person claimed repeatedly that they didn't like to talk to people. I try to reflect back on certain things that each person shares with me, so they get a chance to hear their words from a different perspective. I have found that this helps the grieving person realize that they may be repetitive and in some cases contradicting themselves in some way. When pain is intense, especially the pain of losing a child, people often tell themselves that they will never get past it, they will never heal, they will never be happy again, and that they will never be able to live life fully again. Some of those statements come with caveats, meaning that some of the pain, and feelings of sadness and despair will always remain, but will lessen with time.

People in these intense scenarios often place absolutes on themselves that are unnecessary and are not helpful on their journey to healing. What they are experiencing is referred to as "Vilomah," which means *against the natural order* of things. The parent's natural cycle of life has been disrupted. This can cause intense suffering and often diminishes their hope to live. Support from others is limited because so few perceive the depth or their loss. That is also why I try to be available to those who call me. When "Vilomah" parents first begin to walk in the darkness of their grief, they cannot see anything. But when they are drawn to another "Vilomah" parent, one who can stand with them in the dark, they will begin to learn to see in the dark. Tactfully, I try to encourage them to talk about their loved one, to cry whenever grief comes, and to continue to seek Jesus. One of the saddest mistakes some parents make is, out of their pain, never to speak of their child again. Such silence, far from diminishing the pain, just causes it to build up and may result in life-pervading bitterness. So, let's learn to talk about our pain, because even in our solitude, Jesus is listening.

Psalm 34:18 (NIV), "The Lord is close to the brokenhearted and saves those who are crushed in spirit."

Now I may be exaggerating a bit, but they mentioned at least two dozen times that they didn't like talking to people. I always use reflective listening skills, especially in these types of situations, but I had to chime in after hearing this for the 24th time, "I think you do like to talk to some people because we have now been on the phone for more than an hour. Talking is healing. I want you to talk. I want you to heal. But you keep saying that you don't like to talk to people. I just want to point out that you are lying to yourself. It is never good to lie to ourselves, especially in the throes of grief." At this point the grieving person backpedaled just a bit but agreed that I had shared something true. Then this person openly shared something that was traumatic, possibly criminal, from their childhood. This was something they had endured and the memory of what had happened many years ago surfaced and they began to cry uncontrollably and couldn't put words together.

When they finally collected themselves, they said in a frantic but angry voice, "This was a memory locked in a vault of my mind and the key was thrown away. It was never to be addressed again. And you...you opened it up."

That's when I replied, "When we speak, healing occurs. Sometimes there are things inside of us that come out. Obviously, you needed to release that pain you were holding onto all these years. Releasing that pain may allow you to be more open to healing from the loss of your child. But as I have said to you many times, you might want to consider joining a group because that is what happens when we talk, we heal. I did not open the vault, talking through your pain opened it up."

At this the person became very angry and hung up on me. Almost a week later they called back. The very first thing they said was, "Please forgive me. You were trying to help me. I called you; you did not call me. The things you have said are very helpful and I am grateful that I can call you and know that you will listen. I don't trust many people, but I trust you."

My reply was simply, "You're forgiven."

Jeff Frick

-The impossible choice-

The saddest day of my life is easy to pinpoint. That would be the day that we lost our son, Michael. I could probably write an entire book about the events that occurred between his death and the weeks following his funeral. As you can imagine, my family and I were experiencing many emotions. Those emotions grew excessively because of the dysfunction that resides in my family. For many years, we had been an "event family." What, you may ask, is an event family? An "event family" is a family that *only* comes together when something unusual occurs. Otherwise, there isn't much communication or any at all. In my family, there are two distinct families that are disjointed. One of those families consists of myself and my wife and our children and my brothers, their wives, and their children. My two brothers and I are all from my father's first marriage. The other family consists of my father, his third wife, their two daughters, sons-in-law, and their children. So, whenever these unusual events occur, it is always extremely uncomfortable.

When Michael died, I was the only Christ follower in either family. Although there were all sorts of questions, apprehensions, suspicions, and doubts, I was fully prepared to welcome any and all who wanted to attend my son's funeral. After all, how does one prepare themselves for such an event? For some reason, the four days between my son's death and his funeral seemed like weeks. When everyone started to experience this grueling delay, questions began to form. It wasn't long before I was approached by my two remaining sons and four of my six nieces. Again, I want to reiterate the dysfunction and the pain that afflicted everyone on my side of our unblended family. My sons and nieces asked if Grandpa Ken was going to be allowed in the family hour prior to the public viewing. As you can imagine, from what you've read about my father, I was not prepared to answer such a question.

The next day, my wife and sisters-in-law asked the same question. And finally, my brothers asked as well. Originally, I was not thinking that this was a time for separation or division. But now I was faced with something that made a bad situation even worse. What was I going to do? When everyone on my side of the unblended family approached me as a group, I knew this was not going away. One of the things that I had to take into consideration was that I had made a promise to everyone on my side of the family that we would all cross the bridge together and that I would be the last person behind everyone else. No one was going to be left behind. I made this proclamation because for years my father would play favorites and manipulate anyone who would give him attention. When someone gave him an honest connection, he would exploit it. He never pursued anyone who didn't pursue him. Every person on my side of the family had been wounded repeatedly by him and he didn't seem to care.

So, here I was faced with this impossible choice. If I give my father his way, and allow him to be present in the family hour, how would I deal with the fallout of the people who I was supposed to, and promised to, protect from my father? If I give in to my family's request, I would be excluding my father and anyone else on his side of the family. I wrestled with this decision for almost a day while simultaneously grieving my son. If I am being honest, I was angry at my father for his inaction all these years. Because of his unwillingness, probably inability to apologize to anyone, I was now faced with this dilemma. Although I had grown to forgive my father for the things he had done, no one else on my side had started the journey of forgiving him yet.

So, I sided with my family. I thought that if I could take some of the extra madness from their minds maybe our grieving would be healthier. Since we were already divided and had been for years, this was not going to be the time for unity to happen. I was not going to force them to do something they were not ready to do and make an already uncomfortable situation worse. As you can imagine, there was much tension in the funeral parlor. The people who never paid us any mind suddenly seemed to mind a lot. When everyone on my side received the cold shoulder from everyone on my father's side, I knew that I had made the right choice. He never approached even one of his grandchildren that day. But I still knew that I would need to apologize to him at some point in the future.

When enough time had passed, I reached out to my father. I went to his house, and we talked about that day. As usual, my father didn't have anything to offer me in the way of comfort. I lost a son, but somehow he was the most hurt. I told him that I was sorry for the way that day had unfolded. I asked him for forgiveness. He said something to me that he had said many times before: "Sorry don't mean shit!" I don't know if he ever forgave me because he didn't acknowledge my apology one way or another. He did, however, tell me that he was treated poorly, and that he didn't deserve what I had done to him. That's when I told him about the dilemma that I was facing. I said, "Every person on the other side, not *some* of them, but *all* of them, stated that there was no way that you should be allowed to be present in the family hour."

That's when he got even angrier and said, "Make no mistake. YOU made this choice! YOU did this to me!"

I replied, "Dad, I didn't do this to you. You did this to yourself. This is the direct result of your inaction for the past two decades. All of those people have been wounded by you repeatedly. I have found forgiveness for you, but they are not ready to make that choice yet. So, because you have done nothing, you now sit with nothing. I am not going to choose you over my wife and the two remaining sons that I have."

> *Galatians 6:7-8 (NIV), "Do not be deceived: God cannot be mocked. A man reaps what he sows. Whoever sows to please their flesh, from the flesh will reap destruction; whoever sows to please the Spirit, from the Spirit will reap eternal life."*

-Saying goodbye-

> *Romans 13:8 (NIV), "Let no debt remain outstanding, except the continuing debt to love one another, for whoever loves others has fulfilled the law."*

I have been part of a wonderful ministry at my church for almost 13 years, called the Pastoral Care Team. I remember the leadership team and how welcoming, warm, and caring they are towards the people they are leading. This team always makes me feel well loved, supported and comforted. After a couple years on the team, I was asked if I was interested in taking on more responsibility and filling the role of Peer Group Facilitator. I gladly obliged and was happy to continue learning and growing as a part of the team. Each new position I held with this team carried more responsibility than the position before it. Not only do I enjoy this ministry and the opportunities it has provided me; but I am also grateful that I've been able to see the whole team from a different perspective being the Peer Group Facilitator.

About four years into my time serving as part of this team, I was asked if I, once again, wanted to take on more responsibility. Of course, I agreed. This time, I was becoming part of the leadership team and was sent to a week-long training in a different city. After I returned, my new role began. As part of the leadership team, we often switched roles from year to year to gain a better understanding of how best to serve our team and fulfill our duties. The only role that didn't switch between leaders was the overall leader of the ministry; as this role needed consistency, wisdom and to be led by someone with tenure. To my surprise, during my sixth year on the team I was asked to fill this role.

As with any large team, things are constantly changing as the lives of those who serve on the team continue to change. Filling gaps is an ongoing issue most leaders face on a consistent basis. This is especially true for our Stephens Ministers, due to the high level of commitment that is required of these volunteers. Training for this ministry takes place once a year and consists of 20 modules. Filling gaps is increasingly difficult as it can take quite a bit of time due to the fact that once training begins you must wait six months for the new trainees. Our classes begin in mid-October and finish in early April. However, if for some reason there are no available trainees for a particular year, it takes nearly 18 months to fill a gap. As you can imagine, this can become quite challenging at times.

In my time as leader, I have seen many people come and go. Volunteering is an ebb and flow where few people stay for long periods of time. Because our ministers know the difficulty we face in filling gaps, they are often hesitant to come forward when it has been placed on their hearts to move on from this ministry. I suspect they do this because they don't want to let the team down and/or face confrontation. Whenever I am confronted by a volunteer that is leaving, I can tell almost instantly what they are trying to tell me. Many times, they are beating around the bush to find just the right words and are hoping it won't be awkward. When I get the sense that they are trying to tell me that they are leaving, I quickly say the following words: "Let me apologize to you." "Why are you apologizing to me?" is almost always their response to my apology.

To that I reply, "Please forgive me. You think that I love you only for what you can offer this ministry, and not for simply who you are. I want you to know that wherever God wants you, that's where I want you. If I had loved you well, you would not have been so apprehensive about approaching me to tell me that it's your time to say goodbye. I want you to know how valuable your time here has been for us. If for any reason you would like to return, the doors are always open for you." Upon hearing these words, the response I usually get is something along the lines of, "Thank you for making this easy. I was very nervous to tell you that I was leaving. What a load off my chest." This back and forth has been repeated many times over the years and it always ends the same.

Jeff Frick

-Relationship restored-

What saves a person is taking a step. Then another. And yet another. Our greatest commodity is our time, and our greatest gift is our relationships. If we are unwilling to step toward our greatest gifts by offering our greatest commodity, we will soon know the depths of loneliness and emptiness, which can quickly lead down the road of despair. How many times have you found yourself staring at a broken relationship but are somehow caught in the stalemate of waiting for the other person to do what you are ultimately unwilling to do yourself? Someone must take charge by taking a step, thus saving themselves and the relationship that needs new life. I believe this responsibility lies with the one who is wise. Who is wise, you ask?

> *Luke 2:52 (NIV), "And Jesus grew in wisdom and stature, and in favor with God and man."*

If Jesus had to grow in wisdom, what right do we have to act like a know-it-all? If Jesus accepted greater wisdom, we must never portray ourselves as having arrived, or worse yet, that we are somehow better than another. We learn from others when we humble ourselves and acknowledge how little we actually know. Becoming the student instead of being the teacher is the mark of the truly wise. Who is truly wise, you ask? The wise understand that the more wisdom they attain, the more they realize how much they don't know. Additionally, the wise also know where to focus their thoughts.

> *Romans 16:19 (NIV), "Everyone has heard about your obedience, so I rejoice because of you; but I want you to be wise about what is good, and innocent about what is evil."*

I wasn't always a man of God. Although I walk with Him today, that doesn't mean that I always do the right thing. One thing I can tell you for certain though is that, if it wasn't for God, my relationship with my son Michael would have disintegrated. When I faced that our relationship was on life support, largely because of my doing, it was my faith in God that drew me to take every step possible to show Michael that he was *my* son and that I *loved* him and that I would go to the ends of the earth *for* him. Anything less than that would have resulted in failure. Yes, Michael was lost in the things of this world and living his life in a way that I didn't approve of, but if I wanted to get him back and have any kind of meaningful relationship with him, I had to stop controlling him and start loving him. I had to give my greatest commodity (time) and start taking a step, and then another and yet another to gain my greatest gift (relationship) with Michael. Isn't that how God loves us? Not with control but with reckless love that surpasses our understanding. This love that God lavishes upon us reminds me of some lyrics from a song titled, "Coat of Many Colors" by Brandon Lake. The words are as follows:

Coat of Many Colors
I am clothed in a coat of many colors
I am wrapped in the light
I am held in the arms of a lovin' Father
Was lyin' in a pit, but I'm walkin' the palace now
'Cause once I was a beggar, now I live in the King's house

Because
Red was the blood that saved me
White was the light that pulled me from the dark
Gold was the crown You placed upon my head that showed me who You are
With mercy and grace, I've been embraced like no other
I gave You my heart, You gave me a coat of many colors
Many colors

Hebrews 4:16 (NIV), "Let us then approach God's throne of grace with confidence, so that we may receive mercy and find grace to help us in our time of need."

Michael and I began to spend more time together, and we communicated more. I stopped demanding that he live his life in the way I wanted him to live it and began embracing who my son was. I met him right where he was at. We found genuine connection and our relationship started to flourish. I remember the day Michael looked at me and said, "Dad, you are the wisest man that I know. I love the things you say. I love the way you talk to me. I want you to know that I hear everything you say. I may not be ready to apply it to my life, but please don't ever stop pointing me in the right direction. Thank you, Dad, for making me feel valued." To hear words like that from a once broken, almost dead relationship, will fill your heart with unspeakable joy. Thank you Jesus!

Jeff Frick

(Sketch by Steve Perucca)
Kintsugi Heart

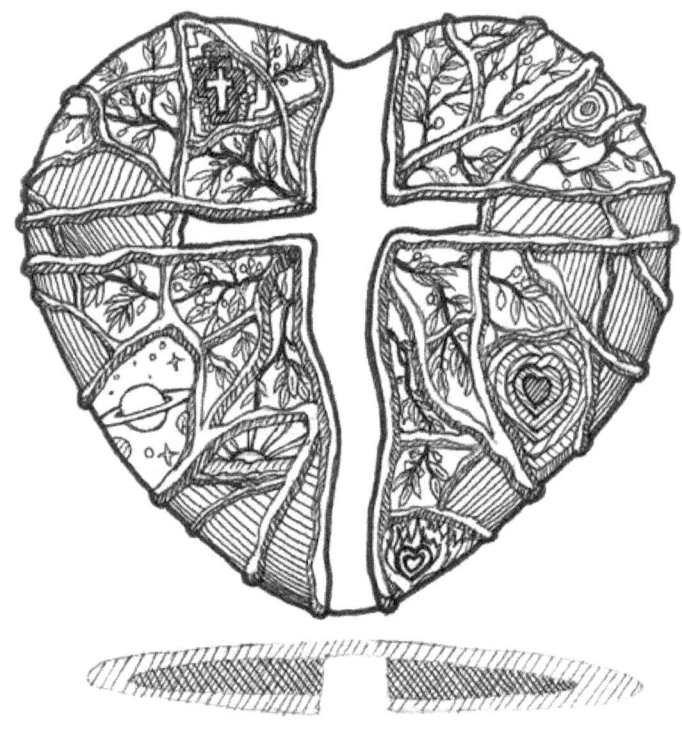

Psalm 147:3 (NIV)
"He heals the brokenhearted and binds up their wounds."

5

I Love You

"Dear children, let us not love with words or speech but with action and in truth."
1 John 3:18 (NIV)

Can you remember the last time you took the time to attempt to understand the depth of the words, "I love you?" Have you ever considered that what we know and understand as love may not feel like or be received as love to the person(s) we are attempting to love? This could be true of one, or some, or of all our relationships at any moment throughout our day. There is a truckload of responsibility and potential for pain we take on when we love another human being. There are dangers of misunderstanding, of betrayal, and of indifference. Yet God calls us to share what we have received; to become broken bread and poured-out wine.

Love "is" a genuine gift we give to others. Love "is not" purchased by another's actions nor is it contingent upon our emotions. Perfect love never considers what it may or may not receive, its only concern is its offering. There are two elements that must exist for love to be present. The first is sacrifice, and the second is free will. God always demonstrates these elements, as His love is a perfect offering. His love excludes none who do not exclude themselves. All who want it may partake of it. It's always offered, because God is love! No matter how long our separation from God, as soon as we turn to Him we receive all that He has for us instantly. He holds nothing back.

John 3:16 (NIV), "For God so loved the world that he gave his one and only Son, that whoever believes in him shall not perish but have eternal life."

There is a song that states, "There's a kind of love that God only knows." The sentence in this song is profoundly true. But the statement "There's a kind of love that God only knows" strikes at the heart of some people and brings offense, because they cannot bear to hear that they aren't loving, or don't love well. Perhaps this is the single greatest reason why the words "I love you" have become so weak and watered down. We spend more time defending our limited ability to love than simply learning to love better. If God is love and we can receive love from Him all the days of our lives due to its endless supply, why do we rest in our understanding of what love is and then stop drawing from His endless supply of it? The fact that we would need to defend our ability to love others well, speaks directly to the lack of love that we currently have come to understand and offer to those we love.

Are you a Christian or a Christ follower? This may give us another clue as to why we have reduced love to mean nothing more than a loose greeting in many cases. A Christian is a wonderful thing to be. It provides security. It provides a sense of peace. It provides a sense of belonging. It says that we believe in Jesus. Christ followers, on the other hand, are known as disciples. Disciples are constant learners under discipline. There is an inherent difference between the two. If you've ever played a video game, think about the anxiety you felt when the background music sped up when your time was almost up to finish your current level. And then, somehow right in the nick of time, you completed the level, the music speed returned to its normal pace, and you received enough coins to catapult your character into the next level. Just like the video game, a new level is granted after you've proven that you're able to take the correct steps, even under the pressure of external forces. One is more likely to become comfortable being uncomfortable as God will always provide a new level of understanding when we are ready to receive. However, this requires a constant seeking and knocking at His door. You don't simply arrive and get comfortable in God's metaphorical La-Z-Boy. Now, I am not saying that every Christ follower is loving people better than any Christian can love people. I am simply pointing out that one tends to be more inclined for growth than the other simply because of their mindset. How we think is important. If a person doesn't know how to think "right," then it's more likely they won't speak "right." If they're not speaking "right," then their words are not being received "right." See the progression?

Perhaps we should begin to use agape love when we talk of God's love and come up with another word for love for human use, because we have butchered the meaning. No one can argue that we have all fallen short of dispersing God's love for His people. With all the conflict and broken relationships among us, it's clear that we haven't even come close to loving others the way God loves us and wants us to love each other.

Romans 5:6-8 (NIV), "You see, at just the right time, when we were still powerless, Christ died for the ungodly. Very rarely will anyone die for a righteous person, though for a good person someone might possibly dare to die. But God demonstrates his own love for us in this: While we were still sinners, Christ died for us."

God's love is unconditional. It's not transactional. God doesn't love you "if" as that would be circumstantial. God doesn't love you "when" as that would be conditional. God loves you "because" He loves You, because He loves You, because He loves You, because He loves You, because He loves You, BECAUSE THAT IS WHAT HE IS LIKE! His love is unconditional! He won't love you any better when you become better! He loves you 100% right now! Even if you have no plans to become better, He will still love you 100%! That's His nature! He loves all the way, all the time! If you and I aren't loving our loved ones in this manner, we have more of God's love to receive. May we not rest in our conditional, transactional, circumstantial, watered down, Hallmark-movie-created, limited understanding of love, but learn to rely on His agape love. I think we can all agree that the world needs more of Him and less of us.

1 John 4:16 (NIV), "And so we know and rely on the love God has for us. God is love. Whoever lives in love lives in God, and God in them."

-Stolen backpack-

Have you ever come across someone who was in need? I think it would be safe to say that we all have encountered someone in need, probably multiple times in our lives. The question is, what did we typically do about it? Surprisingly, the answer to that question may determine the value, or depth, of the *love* that you are attempting to show to the other person. Many of us act like human *doings* instead of human *beings*. We live in a world that tells us we must earn, strive, climb, achieve, and set goals. So, it's no wonder we have become almost robotic doers, as that is the environment where we spend virtually all of our time. We are behavioral beings, and our environment tends to shape our focus. The Scriptures warn us about this.

Ephesians 4:22-24 (NIV), "You were taught, with regard to your former way of life, to put off your old self, which is being corrupted by its deceitful desires; to be made new in the attitude of your minds; and to put on the new self, created to be like God in true righteousness and holiness."

Considering this possibility, I wonder if we ever stop to think about what we are doing when we attempt to help people. Do we give the person what we want them to have? Or do we attempt to find out what they need? There is a vast difference between the two. Giving someone what you want them to have and never caring to find out what they need may be considered a self-serving act of our human *doing*. I know this may seem a bit harsh. But sometimes to get someone's attention, we need to be harsh. We want to open the eyes of those who love to help people but never consider that their help may not be "help" at all.

Consider Hurricane Helene that hit the Southeast United States this past Fall. Considered the deadliest and most devastating hurricane of the 2024 Atlantic hurricane season; Helene tore through multiple states and dumped 42 trillion gallons of rain on the area. I personally know of friends whose first thought was to donate every last stitch of theirs and their children's clothing from their closets that have been waiting to be packed away, in an effort to help the families affected by this deadly season of hurricanes. While you may be thinking what a wonderful idea and how blessed these families will be to receive these gifts, but just how helpful would this genuine act of kindness really be when these families may have just watched their homes float away down the abyss of endless water and debris with no place to even store such donations? While genuine, their kindness and well wishes could be shared with a donation of some sort after contacting the Red Cross or similar entity and finding out what is really needed.

When we never inquire what the person needs and only respond with what we want them to have, we remove their humanity and dignity. We treat them as an inanimate object instead of a living breathing person. It's like we don't even care about the person at all. Have you ever heard the phrase **"Be devoted to Jesus, not the things you believe Jesus might want you to do?"** Giving someone what you want them to have and not finding out what they need is basically the same thing. We are often devoted to doing good things, but they are not always loving. This became a great teaching moment at one of my Bible studies many years ago.

We had a group of men totaling nearly 20 that met weekly at a local coffee shop. Included in this group was a man who was homeless. In the time that this study met, we all got a chance to understand Mike's circumstances. It appeared that living homeless was less hassle, even more attractive, than being with his family because of their crazy situation. I don't know that I agreed with Mike, and I don't know that many of the other men did either. However, it was his life and his decision. Mike was faithful, showing up every week. We all got closer as we dug into the Scriptures.

After we had met for about six months, I was sitting at my computer one morning and noticed several email exchanges between the men in the Bible study. It quickly became evident that Mike's backpack was stolen the night before. Many of the men were angry and anxious and wanted to quickly offer their support. When I read all the emails, these men were planning to lavish Mike with a complete wardrobe. One man said, "I will buy him five shirts."

Another said, "I will buy him five pairs of pants."

Another said, "I will get Mike a couple of pairs of shoes."

Still another said, "I will get his socks and underwear." There were many others who had chimed in to help and if they had succeeded, Mike would have needed to move back into his family's house.

When I interjected, I asked, "Why would you burden Mike with all these clothes?" They started responding one by one. Their emails were filled with anger that someone would do this to their friend. They were angry that Mike had nothing left to his name. They also indicated that as brothers in Christ it was their duty to step into his circumstances. So, I asked the men, "Where do you think Mike is going to put all these clothes that you plan to buy him? Mike doesn't have a dresser or a closet. You are trying to solve Mike's problems through your own eyes instead of looking through Mike's eyes. I notice none of you thought about buying him a backpack. Again, how will any of this help Mike? He may be able to use a couple pairs of pants and a couple shirts, but maybe you should ask Mike what he needs instead of giving him what you want him to have. In this way you will show him that he is seen, heard, and valued. You will love him well, instead of looking past him." Sometimes loving people isn't love at all.

After hearing this, each man said, "I never thought about it that way. Thanks for enlightening me!"

> 1 John 4:7-8 (NIV), "Dear friends, let us love one another, for love comes from God. Everyone who loves has been born of God and knows God. Whoever does not love does not know God, because God is love."

-Not your yes man-

Sometimes loving someone requires us to deliver tough love which doesn't always feel like love to the person who is receiving our tough love. In my first book, "How do I Love my *Neighbor*? 4 PROMISES AND 6 TRUTHS" I make four promises to all the people that God places in front of me. One such promise is that I will never be your "yes man." I will never tell you what you *want* to hear. I will tell you what you *need* to hear. The men that I disciple know this promise well but still sometimes forget.

A man was in my office, and he wanted help and guidance to determine how to solve a relationship problem he was experiencing. He stated that his girlfriend had disrespected him, and he wanted to know how to proceed. So, I asked him to tell me what happened. He stated that he had placed a call to an exterminator because his mother's house had some unwelcome visitors. He had left a message, and he was waiting for a return call. In the meantime, his girlfriend called him on her way home from work. She was upset and crying. Apparently she was contemplating if she should attempt to find a new job because the pressure at her current job was extremely intense. While she was trying to convey what was happening and why she was so upset, he told her that he had another call coming in that he had to answer and hung up. Almost two and a half hours later, he called her back. She told him that she didn't feel like talking at that moment and that she would reach out to him tomorrow. The disrespect he was referring to in our meeting was his girlfriend not wanting to talk later in the day when he called.

> James 1:19-20 (NIV), "My dear brothers and sisters, take note of this: Everyone should be quick to listen, slow to speak and slow to become angry, because human anger does not produce the righteousness that God desires."

I asked the man, "What do you think she did wrong?"

He replied, "She didn't talk to me. She kind of pushed me aside and I didn't like it. I want to know why she refused to talk to me when I called her. I think it's wrong. It makes me feel like we are not as close as I thought we were."

I asked him, "Do you think you had any part in the disrespect that you claim you received? Is there anything else you could have done differently?"

He replied, "All she had to do was talk to me and I probably wouldn't be angry."

> *Proverbs 12:18 (NIV), "The words of the reckless pierce like swords, but the tongue of the wise brings healing."*

After asking him if he was done sharing his story and if there were any other details about this particular event that he wanted to include, he said that was it and wanted my counsel. At this, I said, "You have shared the story in your own words and in the way you want me to hear it. According to you, there are no other pertinent details that could be added. So, based on what you have said, I would side with your girlfriend 1000 times out of 1000 times."

He quickly replied, "I didn't share the story correctly? You didn't hear what I said!"

I replied, "Not only did you tell me the story the way you wanted to, but humans almost always paint themselves in the best light when telling a story, especially when we are talking about conflict of any kind. You need to come to grips that you could have done many things differently."

With a dumbfounded look on his face, "Like what?" is all that he could muster.

I continued, "For starters, you could have informed your girlfriend that you were expecting a call so you could help your mother solve a problem. If the call comes in while we are talking, I will have to answer but I will call you right back. I am sure your girlfriend knows how much your mother means to you, and I am certain she would have agreed. But you didn't give her a heads up. Next, your girlfriend was crying about the difficulty and the pressure from her job. That is not a joke. You could have pressed into her tears more and let her know that you will support her and provide whatever comfort she needs. Lastly, you could have called her back in minutes rather than hours. All these things would have removed your feeling of being disrespected. Can you even imagine how she feels? She's crying and you hang up and don't call her back for hours. How was she supposed to know you were expecting a call if you didn't tell her? I don't blame her for not wanting to talk that night. By the way, did she call you the next morning?"

"Yes," he said. The man looked rather dejected at this point. He couldn't believe that I didn't side with him, that I wouldn't endorse his position.

I told him, "In this case, you were wrong. You need to apologize and make sure she knows how much you love her." As he was leaving, I shared one final statement with him, "I know that you are struggling with this situation. You may not even like what I shared today. But I want you to remember that I have never been your yes man, and I never will. I love you too much and want you to succeed in this relationship with your girlfriend and all your future endeavors. My ceiling is your floor. Never forget that." At this, we parted by hugging, and he knew that I was for him and not against him.

> *Proverbs 17:17 (NIV), "A friend loves at all times, and a brother is born for a time of adversity."*

-Wanting but not receiving-

Ever since the day my son Michael died, God has continued to bring people into my life that I never asked to meet, who have also lost children. I used to wonder why God was doing this. Why has He chosen to use me? But as the numbers kept climbing, with no end in sight, and the circumstances behind my meeting these people became more improbable, I stopped asking and started accepting that there are people who need to be comforted from the hell of losing a child. Some 83 times in five years is not a coincidence.

With the numbers growing, and many in my community knowing my circumstances, some of those *God-sequences* come from referrals. I have received referrals from parents that I have already helped through a loss. I have also received referrals from friends and family that know someone who was thrust into this unimaginable tragedy when they lost their child. I have been called by people who said, "'So and so' said you were the person who could help me." I have prayed with people only to find out through their tears that they are grieving the loss of a child. And, of course, God has even sent me on trips hundreds

The Twelve Most Important Words

and thousands of miles away just so I could interact with someone who He knew needed comforting during such a devastating loss.

One day, a friend of mine approached me about his co-worker. He said, "This man has lost two children and is struggling tremendously. I gave him your number. I hope you don't mind. He will be calling you soon."

I replied, "Of course I don't mind. You can share my number with anyone. If God places a person in front of me, I promised Him I would do my best to love them." I have learned to stop anticipating an immediate response when I am approached with a request like this. As it turned out, God brought two other parents to me before Josh got the nerve to call me.

The weirdest thing happened when Josh called. His first words to me were, "I have spent 15 years in a federal penitentiary."

I quickly replied, "Josh, what are your children's names?" I was amazed at what had just happened, and at the same time overwhelmed with empathy for Josh. Can you imagine walking through life with a feeling like you must announce you were once a felon hoping people won't run away when you tell them? Many people have what I refer to as *scare statements*. They have a fear that if their worst moment in life were exposed, people will run away from them. So, they get it out of the way immediately to see who will leave. It's almost like turning on a light in a barn and watching bugs scatter into the dark corners. This man was trying to grieve the loss of two children, and at the same time hoping that he would be accepted when he introduced himself to someone new. I said, "Josh, you are not defined by your past or your current struggle, you are defined by who you are in Christ. I pray that you can grow to a place where you don't have to announce that you were once a felon with your initial entry. I won't treat you any different. I am sorry that you have felt that rejection because others are holding you to your worst day."

Josh and I began to talk about the difficulty he and his wife were having trying to cope with the second loss. Both of their babies were born and then died shortly thereafter, within hours. At one point, I began to cry with Josh because of the weight he was carrying, and the pain, which I knew all too well, he was dealing with. He said he and his wife were at odds with each other and couldn't come together to grieve or even talk. I explained that grief is challenging and difficult for many reasons, mostly because we tend to shove it way deep down inside, so we don't have to deal with it. But because of the nature of your grief, you will be forced to let it pass through you because this pain isn't going away. It will eventually, with time, change from a constant stabbing to a numbing ache; but make no mistake, it will never go away. This grief will haunt you for life.

With those words, Josh said, "Thank you, Jeff. Thank you for taking my call. Thank you for being available to help."

> *Hebrews 6:10 (NIV), "God is not unjust; he will not forget your work and the love you have shown him as you have helped his people and continue to help them."*

Then Josh shared that he was not receiving the comfort that he felt he needed from his wife. In fact, she was acting in a way that exceeded what he thought was necessary. Basically, her grief didn't look the way he thought it should. Two people who claim to love each other, were denying comfort for the other while wanting the very comfort they were unwilling to give.

I said, "Josh, your wife's grief will look different than yours and yours will look different than mine. Grief is personal, it's like a fingerprint, no two are alike."

That's when he said, "But you don't understand, I am hurting so bad. This is literally killing me, and my wife won't help me." That's when I told Josh about his duty as a man, father, and a husband.

I said, "Josh, men are to lead, guide, protect, and provide. Your wife needs you to be strong. So that requires you to search out the men who can provide for your needs so that you can provide for hers. Life is difficult and the responsibility of caring for our families will be challenged in many ways. I don't want to minimize your pain, but your wife carried those babies for nine months. She has an attachment that you and I will never understand. So as bad as you feel, I guarantee she feels significantly worse. What your wife needs is for you to comfort her and tell her that you love her. She needs to know that you will stand by her no matter what. If you love her, hug her, and tell her, you won't have to say anything else."

Josh thanked me again. He asked if we could talk at some point again in the future. Then he said one more thing, "I want to know that my babies are being cared for and that I will see them again. Will I?"

I replied, "Josh, your babies are in heaven and God is caring for them. Now go comfort your wife and tell her that you love her."

> *1 Thessalonians 4:13-18 (NIV), "Brothers and sisters, we do not want you to be uninformed about those who sleep in death, so that you do not grieve like the rest of mankind, who have no hope. For we believe that Jesus died and rose again, and so we believe that God will bring with Jesus those who have fallen asleep in him. According to the Lord's word, we tell you that we who are still alive, who are left until the coming of the Lord, will certainly not precede those who have fallen asleep. For the Lord himself will come down from heaven, with a loud command, with the voice of the archangel and with the trumpet call of God, and the dead in Christ will rise first. After that, we who are still alive and are left will be caught up together with them in the clouds to meet the Lord in the air. And so we will be with the Lord forever. Therefore encourage one another with these words."*

-Homeiromai-

What if I were to tell you that there are more summits of God's love than we have learned to receive. Would you be willing to allow God to introduce them to you? Far too many of us have learned to remain comfortable with the love that we have received and therefore can only give away whatever understanding of love we currently have. But God's love stretches further than we can comprehend, and many of us, no, most of us, never entertain more.

> *Ephesians 3:14-19 (NIV), "For this reason I kneel before the Father, from whom every family in heaven and on earth derives its name. I pray that out of his glorious riches he may strengthen you with power through his Spirit in your inner being, so that Christ may dwell in your hearts through faith. And I pray that you, being rooted and established in love, may have power, together with all the Lord's holy people, to grasp how wide and long and high and deep is the love of Christ, and to*

> *know this love that surpasses knowledge—that you may be filled to the measure of all the fullness of God."*

I found *more* one day while researching for a Bible study. I typically filter through about 20 different references to ensure a good representation of the scriptures that we would be studying. On this particular day, I wasn't finding what I felt was enough information to fill our 60-minute study session. So I went to another resource, one that I rarely use. To my amazement, God provided revelation knowledge that I desperately needed. We were studying 1 Thessalonians, Chapter two, verses six through eight. Verse eight instantly became one of my favorite verses because of what God revealed to me.

> *1 Thessalonians 2:8 (NIV), "so we cared for you. Because we loved you so much, we were delighted to share with you not only the gospel of God but our lives as well."*

The word love as it is used in this verse translates to a phrase: *affectionately desirous*. What did Paul mean when he said he was "affectionately desirous" of the believers in Thessalonica? This phrase is taken from the Greek word *homeiromai*, and this word is extremely important because it tells us a lot about the heart of the apostle Paul. The word *homeiromai* was primarily found on the grave markers of children that had died, and it describes what these parents felt for their child. It indicates a deep longing or an affectionate, fervent desire to see the child one more time.

By using this word, Paul was conveying his deep desire to see these Thessalonian believers one more time. He loved them very much, and like a parent who longs to see their child who has died, just one more time; everything within the apostle Paul longed to be able to visit the church of Thessalonica and minister again face to face to these believers whom he held so close to his heart.

Having lost a child myself, and living with an unsettled, constant numbing pain stirring in my soul, this verse provided comfort that I never thought I would experience. God longs to be with us. Like a parent who has lost a child, the moment we turn our eyes away from Him and back to ourselves, God longs to be with us. *Homeiromai* is His offering to us. The amazing thing about this verse that Paul penned is that he had only known this group of believers in Thessalonica for three weeks before persecution caused him to leave. Can you imagine the love that he had for people if this was the expression he would convey after only knowing them for three weeks?

My immediate reaction after God revealed this knowledge to me was why are we waiting to give this kind of love to people until after they die? Paul was spreading it out after three weeks. Why are we not doing the same? Part of the reason is that we, in our current society, have reduced love to something totally devoid of its actual meaning. Instead of sharing the sentiments of love in a meaningful way, we say, "I love my house. I love my car. I love my spouse. I love pizza." There is no true distinction in the way we use the word love. In fact, we say we *love* almost anything and everything. It's clear to me that we have all been conditioned to say the word love, similar to a greeting of, "How are you", that we don't really mean and hope the other person doesn't respond?

When I first discovered the amazing revelation of this morsel of *more* of God's expansive love, I began sharing it with the men that I disciple. I remember sharing it with one particular man and he responded, "Yes! Of course! I give this away every day to every person."

I asked him, "Are you sure? Because you had never heard the word *homeiromai* until just a few seconds ago. You didn't know the meaning or the depth, but somehow you give that away to every person? Have you lost a child? Interesting." It was that exchange that revealed to me why love has been reduced to something far less than what it was intended to be. We have convinced ourselves that we have the market cornered on how to express love. God couldn't possibly teach us anything, because we already know it all.

I now include the God-given revelation knowledge of *homeiromai* at every funeral service that I preside over. Every person in the gallery is experiencing *homeormai* for their loved one, but they don't know it. The comfort that comes with applying a name to our longing and fervent desire to see our loved one again is something that only God could have foreseen and supplied. God's love is so expansive. If we would just humble ourselves, we would be able to share the words "I love you" in such a more beautiful and intentional way.

Jeff Frick

-Sons and daughters-

When my wife and I were starting our family, we didn't really care so much whether we had a boy or a girl because we just wanted healthy children. We would spend an equal amount of energy deciding on boy names versus girl names. After three pregnancies, we had three wonderful sons. We contemplated thoughts about pregnancy one last time in hopes of having a girl, however, after a few months of careful thought and prayer, we decided that our three sons were the answers to our prayers regarding the idea of having more children. Besides, if we were to have another child, we would probably have another boy as it seems we were destined to have boys. All kidding aside, we love our sons and wouldn't trade what we have for anything. They were then, and still are today, the greatest blessings from God.

My brothers are girl dads. Whenever we would come together for family meals, adventures, vacations, or just to hang out, there would always be a sort of confusion between my brothers and I. This confusion stemmed from the difference between my boys and their girls. My boys were typical boys that were always wrestling and rough housing. On the other side, my nieces were quieter, calmer, not so willing to be dangerous in the way that they played games in the yard. Their demeanor was laid back, cool, calm and collected as opposed to my sons being loud and in your face. For my brothers and I, this was always something we needed to account for when we got together. I think it was a bit easier for my brothers, because the way my sons acted was almost exactly the way we had acted when we were younger. It was sort of natural, even normal and quite nostalgic.

Still, my wife and I always held onto the thought that we would have loved to have had a daughter. What we somehow always seemed to forget, was that one day we would be blessed by having daughters come into our lives in a different way. God would bring our family these gifts in His time. My wife and I started our family in 1995, and 25 years later, He would bring us Rachael, our oldest son, Matthew's wife. Four years after that, God brought us Julia, our youngest son, David's wife. Sadly, our middle son, Michael didn't live long enough to take a wife.

> *Ecclesiastes 3:11 (NIV), "He has made everything beautiful in its time. He has also set eternity in the human heart; yet no one can fathom what God has done from beginning to end."*

The Twelve Most Important Words

It always amazes me how God demonstrates His glory and how He is redeeming the events of our lives and changing our circumstances that make way for legacies to be born. While growing up, I was forced to live through multiple divorces because my parents were searching for their own happiness. I always hated the awkwardness of meeting new people and wondering how long they would be part of my life, and all the while attempting to develop a trusting relationship. I swore that I would never bring a child into such an environment. My wife and I tried our best to bring wholeness into our sons' lives. On the days that Rachael and Julia entered our lives, a new definition of wholeness was experienced by us all. For many people, what I have just shared might not seem so special, but I'll explain why it is indeed so special to us.

God knew that my wife and I desired having daughters. He knew that with three sons we would be hopeful for three daughters someday. He also knew that our son Michael would have an abbreviated life. So, what did God do? God brought us two of the most beautiful, talented, energetic, funny, witty, kind, loving, empathetic, thoughtful, confident, honest, intelligent, patient, strong, supportive, and humble daughters. In a single word, they are temperate. They can enter any space or circumstance and bring comfort to anyone at any time. During a time when we were still deeply grieving the loss of our son Michael, they were salve to our aching hearts. They brought a new level of joy into our hearts that we desperately needed. But most of all, they love our sons, they make them happy, and our sons love them. My wife and I have told both of these beauties on multiple occasions that we love them simply because they love our sons. We don't need another reason. But we have more reasons than we can possibly share in one lifetime.

Could the story of our relationship with these beautiful daughters of ours get any better? Well yes, it could! We are so blessed to be able to truly enjoy sharing our time and space with these women and their parents. I don't know how many people can say that they regularly have meals with their children's in-laws, but we do. I don't know how many people take vacations with their children's in-laws, but we do. I don't know how many people can say they regularly help out with household projects with their children's in-laws, but we do. In fact, we don't use the suffix in-law with our daughters, we just call them our daughters. They are truly part of our family. We don't want any kind of separation to ever come between us, so we don't even use words that would invoke that they were not always a part of our family. We are staples in each other's lives, and my wife and I are so grateful that the desire in our hearts to have daughters that we've carried with us all this time has been granted.

The closeness that we get to share today is the polar opposite of what my childhood was like. God is in the redeeming business if you are willing to walk with Him. You won't know when or how He will do it, but His way will be better than you could have ever imagined. At the time of writing this book, our oldest daughter Rachael is expecting her second child, and our youngest daughter Julia is expecting her first. We will be grandparents for a third time. The best thing is that we get to share this joy with our daughters' parents.

> *Psalm 37:3-4 (NIV), "Trust in the Lord and do good; dwell in the land and enjoy safe pasture. Take delight in the Lord, and he will give you the desires of your heart."*

> *Psalm 66:16-20 (NIV), "Come and hear, all you who fear God; let me tell you what he has done for me. I cried out to him with my mouth; his praise was on my tongue. If I had cherished sin in my heart, the Lord would not have listened; but God has surely listened and has heard my prayer. Praise be to God, who has not rejected my prayer or withheld his love from me!"*

I cry every time I am reminded of what God has done and the blessings He has bestowed upon us. We never miss an opportunity to tell our sons and daughters we love them. I pray they never grow weary of hearing it either.

> *Philippians 1:3-4 (NIV), "I thank my God every time I remember you. In all my prayers for all of you, I always pray with joy."*

-The hidden blessings of God-

I believe some of our biggest shortcoming's stem from not training our minds to remain present with God. Most of us never come to the realization that we are behavioral and that our behaviors permeate every area of our life, but often in different ways. A prime example is remaining present with God instead of looking forward, backward, left, or right. Guilt and shame keep us caught in yesterday; fear and worry have us living in tomorrow. Somehow we get so focused on the edges, we forget the Center. God's Word says don't look left or right but remain focused on Him. When we are focused on the

Center, we care *not* where the edges are. But when we focus on the edge our only concern is how far we can move it for our liking to fit our agenda. God's peace is in the present. His blessings are to be experienced in the present. So why do we refuse to walk with God and instead take our own journeys? Because in doing so, we prevent ourselves from seeing and experiencing some of His greatest blessings.

> *Isaiah 45:3 (NIV), "I will give you hidden treasures, riches stored in secret places, so that you may know that I am the Lord, the God of Israel, who summons you by name."*

If I had not remained focused on God, my relationship with my son Michael would have never been restored. I never saw it until He revealed it to me, but God brought one of the greatest blessings out of the darkest times in my life. I had no idea that "time" was of the essence, but God *did*. It's so scary when I look back at it and realize that if I had brushed off the nudge God was giving me, I would have missed out on any type of reconciliation with Michael. Thinking about that is too much to bear. Thankfully, I can think back to the nudge I felt and see the countless pieces that had been strung together knowing that none of it could have ever been possible without His hand on *every single piece*. I'm so grateful that God worked on my heart and gave me a willing spirit to not only hear Him and follow through with initiating contact with Michael, but also that He spoke into Michael, whether he knew it or not, and softened his heart to accept the apology that put into motion the reconciliation we experienced as father and son. Because of this, my relationship with Michael became as strong as it had ever been. That didn't mean that Michael was living the life that his mother and I had dreamt for him. In fact, just the opposite was true. We wouldn't see or hear from Michael for many days at a time, and he rarely responded to our text messages. Still, when he was ready to come around, he always texted me, usually asking me to give him a haircut. Whenever we saw each other, we hugged and we said, "I love you." That might seem normal to many of you, and it should be, but it wasn't always normal for us.

When our sons were younger, we had what many would consider a normal household. As any well written book has a plot twist, so did our household. Somewhere around the age of 16, Michael had changed. I remember one night when Michael was threatening to move out and never come back, our house was so shaken that night that my youngest son David was at my feet, begging me, and crying out, "Please Dad! Please! Don't let this happen!" He was so concerned for his brother, Michael. However, about a year later, that same son said, "Get this bum out of here. I can't believe you are still allowing this behavior to go on." The police were frequently at our front door looking for Michael but, again, he was rarely home. Our relationship was rapidly deteriorating because I was too busy looking for answers within myself instead of devoting myself to the Answer Giver. I was so focused on the edge; I forgot the Center. When I gave the circumstance to God, God did what only God could do. Slowly but steadily, progress began to bring us together.

The next four years saw our relationship moving in the right direction. Michael began attending more family functions. We would have dinner at his place of work, which would give us a chance to visit. All three sons planned a trip to the tattoo parlor to honor my wife and I successfully battling cancer, without either of us knowing about it. They presented their tattoos to us at the same time. Each one was uniquely different from the other, but all the same. We were so overjoyed that our sons were together, we didn't care that they had gotten tattoos. Michael and I would spend time together sharing meals and talking about life. All the things that families do; we were beginning to do. My wife and I started thinking, even believing, that things were going to return to the way that they once were.

Because of Michael's lifestyle, he was rarely ever in our home and had no real place of residency, which left him drifting from one friend's house to another. My wife and I were made to wear a heavy coat of worry and fear for many years because of the lifestyle he chose. A coat of worry that weighed us down, made us cry, kept us from experiencing real joy, shackled us to our greatest fears, and weakened us in a debilitating way. Because of the wonderful changes that were occurring, we began thinking that our heavy coats would be removed forever. One day, the heavy coats of fear and worry were removed, only not in the way my wife and I would have ever wanted. Our greatest fear had come true: Michael was dead. Our heavy coats were removed, only we would have done anything to put them back on. **Anything!** We had no idea that "time" was of the essence. *But God did.*

There is a song that asks a question… "How do you find joy at a good man's wake?" This is only possible if you focus on the Center instead of the edge. It's only possible if you are present with God. God had spared us from having to live the rest of our days constantly questioning why we squandered our chance to restore our relationship with Michael. We could have lived like tomorrow is promised, like time was not of the essence, like Michael will get his life together at some point, but we didn't. We didn't, because of God.

> *James 4:13-15 (NIV), 'Now listen, you who say, "Today or tomorrow we will go to this or that city, spend a year there, carry on business and make money." Why, you do not even know what will happen tomorrow. What is your life? You are a mist that appears for a little while and then vanishes. Instead, you ought to say, "If it is the Lord's will, we will live and do this or that."'*

We live with a grief that is a torture like none other because our son is gone. We don't, however, have to suffer all our days living with guilt because of what we could have done but never did. We take the greatest joy knowing that Michael loved us, and we loved him. These were not empty greetings; they were deep and heartfelt. They were greetings of love that came from the brink of disaster. They had restorative power attached to them. And God's hidden blessings were never needed more than they were at this time of deep, unrelenting sorrow. Praise the Lord!

(Sketch by Steve Perucca)

Proverbs 3:3-4 (NIV)
"Let love and faithfulness never leave you; bind them around your neck, write them on the tablet of your heart. Then you will win favor and a good name in the sight of God and man."

6

Walls Eliminated?

> "My actions built walls
> brick by brick
> one by one
> I've caused them all.
> I want them to fall,
> to change is my call.
> Is it too late? Is this my fate?
> I change my action
> will it change their reaction?"
> -Author Unknown

Colossians 3:12-14 (NIV), "Therefore, as God's chosen people, holy and dearly loved, clothe yourselves with compassion, kindness, humility, gentleness and patience. Bear with each other and forgive one another if any of you has a grievance against someone. Forgive as the Lord forgave you. And over all these virtues put on love, which binds them all together in perfect unity."

If one could see what mankind could be, look at Jesus! All colors and races meet in Him, as the rivers meet the sea. Only in the Kingdom of God do you find diversity in unity and unity in diversity. In God's Kingdom, intrinsic value is placed upon each person. God loves each of us as if there were no other people on the planet. Each of us is given different gifts and talents but every person has the same intrinsic value in the Kingdom of God. No one is more important than the next. We can grow in the Lord all the days of our lives, taking on more and more of His divine nature as we walk with Him. **Ultimately, what we learn to receive from God is on full display every day in every interaction.** There is no need to fake it because everyone is a spectator. We must never forget that with God as our

Source, there is always more. The only end to our receiving is when we stop seeking, knocking, and asking.

> *Psalm 1:1-3 (NIV), "Blessed is the one who does not walk in step with the wicked or stand in the way that sinners take or sit in the company of mockers, but whose delight is in the law of the Lord, and who meditates on his law day and night. That person is like a tree planted by streams of water, which yields its fruit in season and whose leaf does not wither—whatever they do prospers."*

There are no perfect Christians. In fact, there are no perfect people at all. None of us have any excuse for not continually growing in the Fruit of God's Spirit. Maybe that's why we find so much division in our world and in our relationships. We are drawing from an inadequate source. The answers are never going to be found within ourselves.

> *2 John 1:9 (NIV), "Anyone who runs ahead and does not continue in the teaching of Christ does not have God; whoever continues in the teaching has both the Father and the Son."*

I pray that Jesus would be Lord of every person's life, and that one day we would love in the way that He does. Many have said that we don't need God, Jesus, or the Holy Spirit. In fact, there was a song written by John Lennon many years ago called "Imagine." In the lyrics, it asks us to imagine no heaven, imagine people living in peace, and the world living as one. I am here to proclaim that apart from Jesus none of those things are possible. Jesus even asks that His Father's will be done on earth as it is in Heaven.

> *Matthew 6:9-13 (NIV), "This, then, is how you should pray: 'Our Father in heaven, hallowed be your name, your kingdom come, your will be done, on earth as it is in heaven. Give us today our daily bread. And forgive us our debts, as we also have forgiven our debtors. And lead us not into temptation, but deliver us from the evil one.'"*

To those who believe that Jesus is not the Answer, I simply ask one question: If that is true, why do we continue to hurt each other and erect walls that separate us?

-When the real work begins-

Romans 12:9-10 (NIV), "Love must be sincere. Hate what is evil; cling to what is good. Be devoted to one another in love. Honor one another above yourselves."

How many times have you found yourself in a situation where you were in some kind of dispute, fight, or disagreement with a friend or loved one? My guess is that this is all too common of an occurrence in your life. I know it has been in my life. Through my own personal experience, and after listening to literally hundreds of men and women who have found themselves in such a circumstance, I have found that the hardest thing is not swallowing your pride or speaking the 12 most important words, if we even know what the words mean. The hardest thing is the work that follows once we have uncovered the walls that separate us. How do we break down the walls of separation?

Maybe you have swallowed your pride and have spoken the 12 most important words. After doing that, did you think that everything would be better and that it would somehow be fixed just because you said some nice words? Or did you find that somehow there is still distance between you and your loved one that is causing you still to be separated? Why is this distance still between you? The answer is found in your demonstration, or lack thereof, regarding the nice words you spoke and the momentary ball of fire, otherwise known as your pride, you swallowed like the hot sauce you were dared to eat by your buddies when you were a teenager. Have you attempted to change the behavior that caused the dispute? If not, then why? Didn't you say the 12 most important words? Our changed behavior will always serve as the proof our friends or loved ones need to see that we truly mean what we say. Our words have little value if they are not followed by real change.

Some of us say the 12 most important words to someone we have wronged just to make the problem go away. We really don't mean what we say, we just want peace at any cost. It is never really about the so-called value we place on the other person, or the love we claim to have for them. For some of us, it's always about…us. We have little to no regard for what the other person needs or wants. We manipulate instead of love, to get our way. Perhaps this "bait and switch" has been successful with some people in our lives, so we exploit it to its fullest for as long as they allow us to get away with it. We recited the 12 most important words knowing full well that we really didn't mean them, and somehow the other person seemed to eat it up. But what are we to do when our manipulative tactics aren't so successful and our lack of concern for anyone other than ourselves is on full display? What then?

What I hope we all come to understand is that while our manipulation may provide us with a false sense of comfort and peace that allows us to cling to the idea that all is well in our relationship; however, there is something unsettling stirring in the background. The same person we have been manipulating; has also been the subject of our disrespect and hurt. Every time we say words we don't mean, to get what we want, a brick is laid in an invisible wall that is building between us and the person we are hurting. This invisible wall is fashioned over time for the protection of the person we have been continuously wounding. In many cases, this wall only becomes visible, or evident to us, when our manipulation no longer works. By the time the bricks begin to stack up high enough that we can no longer see each other, the wall of protection is thick, tall, fortified, and strong. The person we have wounded begins to retreat from the relationship and leaves us alone with our empty words. The person we have manipulated is hurt deeply and will no longer allow our bad behavior to slowly destroy them. This is when the real work begins…when you're honest with yourself and are ready to really swallow the ball of fire that is your pride this time!

The real work begins when we are no longer in charge of what our relationship looks like or the intimacy level we would like to experience with the person we have hurt. Only then can our changed behavior and the unknown time frame of our demonstrated behavior change lead us to a hopeful reunion with the person we have harmed. We must be willing to demonstrate that we have changed until…until the person we have harmed learns to trust us again.

Ultimately, we become a new person because of our behavior change and our desire to show the person we harmed that we are serious about changing our behavior, that they are important to us and that we value them and the relationship we are working to restore. Be ready and willing to demonstrate your changed behavior for as long as necessary. Keep in mind that your manipulation didn't build the wall between you overnight, so it wouldn't be fair to expect the wall to come crumbling down overnight either.

Friend, tread lightly if you feel you should be able to ask someone to do something for you that you are not willing to do for another person. Go back to square one if you feel old behaviors creeping in that threaten to erect the wall built by one manipulative brick after another. May we never forget that walls are dangerous! There's an old saying, "Treat others the way you want to be treated." If you don't, walls will form.

-The 3 responses to walls-

Hebrews 12:14 (NIV), "Make every effort to live in peace with everyone and to be holy; without holiness no one will see the Lord."

What do we do when we finally discover that there is a wall with our name on it? Walls are produced because we harm people that we claim to care about and love. We have either never spoken the 12 most important words to our loved one, or we have spoken the 12 most important words, but we lacked an appropriate follow through in terms of changed behavior. The following musing from my friend, Loren Siffring, can help us better understand walls more clearly.

Guard Your Lips!
As you walk through your days, you have choices galore.
When you are with folks who have needs
To give what you have to fill in their gaps,
They will often remember your deeds.
Sometimes it will be that the things that you give
Are not goods, but a promise you make.
This two-part gift will be measured, for sure
Is your follow-through truth or a fake?
When you've given your word, it may cause you some hurt
To deliver the goods like you spoke.
It will measure you, man, so be careful to speak
"Your word is your bond"...That's no joke!
The best gift you can ever give to a wife, son or daughter
Is a promise that's kept, like it's spoken.
A wall is produced that is hard to remove
Whenever a promise is broken.

Jeff Frick

> To be 'quick to hear' and 'slow to speak'
> Will determine the words that come out.
> Once spoken, the fruit they bear will be seen
> To produce life, love and light, but not doubt.

Perhaps you are like most people. We walk through life developing behaviors. These behaviors help us navigate our lives and usually serve us well…until they don't. How do we respond when our behaviors aren't serving us well? It is my belief that we have only three possible responses after discovering there is a wall with our name on it. How we respond will determine if the current relationship, which is clearly in jeopardy, has a chance of being redeemed. Furthermore, our choice of responses will also determine how willing we are to develop new behaviors that will cultivate deeper relationships with others moving forward.

Response No. 1: So, you have discovered that there is a wall with your name on it. The **first** response you can exercise is to forever and completely walk away from the person who has built the wall. This response is an indication that you have decided that this person isn't really as valuable to you as you once thought. You are not willing to put the effort into redeeming the relationship, so therefore you cast this person aside. You are not willing to employ the 12 most important words to assist you in redeeming the relationship you once had with this person. To the person who built the wall, this response would not only be hurtful, but puzzling. If there weren't shared feelings and emotions between the two of you, why would it have been necessary to build the wall of protection in the first place? This response would ensure that the relationship remains damaged forever and would not provide a solid footing to guarantee that this same mistake wouldn't happen again with another person.

Response No. 2: So, you have discovered that there is a wall with your name on it. The **second** response you can exercise is to blame the person who has built the wall. This response is also an indication that you have decided that this person isn't really as valuable to you as you once thought. You are not willing to put the effort into redeeming the relationship and instead of walking away from the person, you blame them solely for all your problems. You are now angry that this person will no longer put up with your callous behavior. You see this relationship as the other person needing to make the necessary adjustments to accommodate you. Again, to the person who built the wall, this response would also be hurtful and puzzling. The person who built the wall cannot understand why you would be so willing to hurt them and not only refuse to take responsibility, but to say that it was their fault for protecting themselves from your bad behavior. This response would also ensure that the relationship would remain damaged forever and would not provide a solid footing to guarantee that this same mistake wouldn't happen again with another person.

Response No. 3: So, you have discovered that there is a wall with your name on it. The **third** response you can exercise is the response that most everyone would like to see from someone who has wronged them, even if it was unintentional. This response is to share the 12 most important words, which are: I was wrong. I am sorry. Please forgive me. I love you. The 12 most important words hold a lot of weight when they are spoken from a true place of remorse and regret for the pain we inflicted due to our poor behavior. Saying these four small phrases can be the difference between losing a relationship and saving it. Let's dig into the meat and potatoes, if you will, of these impactful words:

I was wrong: Three words. I. WAS. WRONG. Three simple words that independently are so easy to say, but yet when put together as a phrase, can be some of the hardest words someone may ever speak. These words are hard for so many to say because when you say them, you're admitting that something you have done was wrong. You're taking responsibility for your actions and are acknowledging that you've impacted them negatively. They aren't easy words to say but can sometimes be almost an immediate relief for both parties, when they are shared wholeheartedly. Admitting you were wrong almost always opens the line of communication for deeper work to be done to mend what is broken.

I am sorry: Ego threatening words to say sometimes as the wrongdoer, but life-giving words to hear as the recipient. There is power in saying you're sorry to a person that you care about. I am sorry translates to: I deeply regret my actions toward you because even though my actions have harmed you, you are valuable to me. One thing to keep in mind when using this phrase is to never follow up "I am sorry" with *"but."* I am sorry for _____, *"but"* you _____ doesn't show regret for our actions, instead it is justifying our actions and holds no place in a heartfelt apology.

Please forgive me: Please don't hang on to the ways I've hurt you, but instead please extend me your grace despite the fact that I cannot undo what has harmed you. Asking to be forgiven shows the person you hurt that you want to redeem and restore the relationship that has been severed because the relationship is worth the work that will be needed for proper restoration. This relationship is too important to me to not seek grace and redemption.

I love you: We can love a lot of things, but a lot of the things we "love," can't love us back. Our car, our home, the perfect cup of coffee, our job, our title, our experiences-and the list goes on, are things we "love," but don't have the capacity to love us in return. Love is far too easy a word to throw around to define our general delight in something. Love is more than that. Love is the cross. I charge you to never take for granted the opportunity to reiterate to the person you have hurt that you love them. That they are prized and valued in your sight regardless of the turmoil they are facing because of your poor actions. Your actions in the moment you hurt them obviously didn't convey your love for them; but with your flaws, mistakes, and all, express your desire for relationship restoration through heartfelt love and determination that ensures they feel it.

> *John 13:34-35 (NIV), "A new command I give you: Love one another. As I have loved you, so you must love one another. By this everyone will know that you are my disciples, if you love one another."*

Your changed behavior will always undergird these words as meaningful to the person that was harmed. Remember, our words have little value if not followed by our demonstration of changed behavior and patterns.

Looking at the three responses to walls outlined above, one could argue that the first response is the worst response. We could determine that the result of throwing a relationship away, basically getting rid of a person we claimed to value and love, is heartless. In reality, the second response is actually harsher than the first. It is the harsher of the two responses because we know we have the power to remove our loved one's pain. All we have to do is humble ourselves and take action steps to show them that they are valuable to us. Instead, in this response we refuse to take action. Perhaps we enjoy watching people suffer? Perhaps our understanding of love is deeply skewed? Perhaps we are so selfish we don't know how to love someone besides ourselves? Watching someone suffer and taking no action to alleviate their suffering when we have the power to remove it is nothing short of sinister. Why do we derive pleasure from this type of behavior? Self-protection always places the relationship at a far distant second. Where there is self-protection, there will always be very tall walls.

Why are walls so dangerous? Why should we try earnestly to keep walls from forming? Why should we do everything within our power to remove whatever walls exist currently in our relationships? Simply put, walls are dangerous because they separate us. Let's pretend that you find yourself in a relationship that isn't as close as you would like it to be. After analyzing said relationship, it becomes evident to you that there is a wall with your name on it. You do the right and best thing by responding with the 12 most important words: *"I was wrong. I am sorry. Please forgive me. I love you."* You change your behavior and over time you win the trust of the person who built the wall. Course by course, brick by brick, the wall is eventually removed. At this point we can be lulled into thinking that the work of restoring the relationship is complete. That would be an incorrect assumption on our part.

The reason walls are so dangerous is because the scar from the wounds that created the wall in the first place will always remain with the person we mistreated. In the event that our poor behavior surfaces again and becomes evident to the person we have harmed, the wall that once separated us will return instantly. This time, there will not be the courtship of hoping that our behavior changes. We have already proven that we have the potential to harm this person we claim to love. They have already been afflicted by our callousness. This time, they will not be offering us grace. Now the work of restoring the relationship becomes even harder than before. Walls are not something to play games with because people should matter to us for no other reason than people matter to God.

-Psalm 139-

Have you ever had a moment in your faith journey where God shared something with you that in that moment a lifetime of ills became instantly healed and life took on different meaning? I was blessed to have one of these moments just a few short years ago. This moment with God, which can only be characterized as holy and divine, has opened doors to my faith that I didn't know were previously closed. The book that you are reading right now is a byproduct of this insightful and beautiful moment that continues to amaze me.

Jeff Frick

> *Romans 8:28 (NIV), "And we know that in all things God works for the good of those who love him, who have been called according to his purpose."*

To make the words of Romans 8:28 come alive as something that would change my life forever, God used Psalm 139 in the most beautiful way. A couple of years ago, I went to a friend's house to attend his home church. When I arrived, my friend informed me that he had invited a guest speaker to share the message that day. This speaker was a pastor from out of town and operated a ministry in the western United States. After the speaker introduced himself and allowed everyone a chance to ask their most pertinent questions in regard to his ministry, he informed us that we would be breaking down Psalm 139. Upon hearing this, my response was, "Of course we are!"

A few months earlier, I was sitting in my weekly Bible study when one of the men said that he had a request for us. He was hoping that we would participate in writing a letter to his daughter who was going to be graduating law school later that year. He informed us that he had been highlighting verses and writing notes in the margins of the Bible that he was carrying and that the Bible was a present for his daughter. He stated that he was going to be presenting the Bible, and any letters we write, at Christmas when he and his wife went to visit her at college. I knew that I was going to write his daughter a letter, and I knew that I had quite a bit of time, about four months, to consider what I would write to her. For some reason, I believe God inspired me because I had an overwhelming urge one Sunday morning to sit down and write the letter. In the letter I included parts of Psalm 139.

Imagine my surprise when I arrived at my friend's home church to find out that we would be studying Psalm 139 on the same morning that I would write a letter that I had more than four months to write but felt inspired to write on the same Sunday and included verses from Psalm 139. Can you even calculate the odds? I highly doubt it! This was not a coincidence. This was God all the way. But the story gets even better. The guest speaker began to break down Psalm 139.

> *Psalm 139 (NIV), 'You have searched me, Lord, and you know me. You know when I sit and when I rise; you perceive my thoughts from afar. You discern my going out and my lying down; you are familiar with all my ways. Before a word is on my tongue you, Lord, know it completely. You hem me in behind and before, and you lay*

your hand upon me. Such knowledge is too wonderful for me, too lofty for me to attain. Where can I go from your Spirit? Where can I flee from your presence? If I go up to the heavens, you are there; if I make my bed in the depths, you are there. If I rise on the wings of the dawn, if I settle on the far side of the sea, even there your hand will guide me, your right hand will hold me fast. If I say, "Surely the darkness will hide me and the light become night around me," even the darkness will not be dark to you; the night will shine like the day, for darkness is as light to you. For you created my inmost being; you knit me together in my mother's womb. I praise you because I am fearfully and wonderfully made; your works are wonderful, I know that full well. My frame was not hidden from you when I was made in the secret place, when I was woven together in the depths of the earth. Your eyes saw my unformed body; all the days ordained for me were written in your book before one of them came to be. How precious to me are your thoughts, God! How vast is the sum of them! Were I to count them, they would outnumber the grains of sand— when I awake, I am still with you. If only you, God, would slay the wicked! Away from me, you who are bloodthirsty! They speak of you with evil intent; your adversaries misuse your name. Do I not hate those who hate you, Lord, and abhor those who are in rebellion against you? I have nothing but hatred for them; I count them my enemies. Search me, God, and know my heart; test me and know my anxious thoughts. See if there is any offensive way in me, and lead me in the way everlasting.'

I will paraphrase what the guest speaker said in the 90 minutes that followed. He said, "God knows us. God is so big that no person could comprehend Him. There is no place we can flee from God's Spirit or Presence. Each of us is wonderfully made. God knew us before we ever came to be. We are all given a set number of days. God's thoughts for us cannot be numbered. God will lead us in the way everlasting." When the guest speaker finished breaking down Psalm 139, he said, "Since you now know that God has always been with us from the beginning, close your eyes and think of a time in your childhood when a traumatic event happened. When you have the moment in your mind, look for God. When the moment originally occurred you couldn't see God, even though He was there. But now you will find God in that moment, so look for God because he was there."

Instantly, I was drawn to the night my father left. I was nine years old. I remembered the moment vividly. I remembered crying myself to sleep. Then I remembered the next morning I went across the street to the Parks and Recreation Department. I remembered not feeling well, feeling sad, feeling lonely, feeling isolated, feeling lost, feeling broken, feeling unwanted. I remember one of the volunteers approaching me and asking if everything was all right. He said, "Are you okay? You look like you've lost your best friend."

I told him that my father had left us last night. He then suggested we go for a walk. We must have walked around that park 10-12 times that day. I think we walked for hours. This man, someone who cared enough to notice, someone who cared enough to ask questions, someone who cared enough to lend me his ear, this man gave me his time. I remembered feeling lighter, less heavy, from the pain that I was experiencing. This man from across the street, someone I didn't know before this traumatic event and someone I forgot after this incident, was suddenly in my mind as I was remembering the trauma from my childhood, while looking for God.

That's when God spoke to me more clearly than He had ever spoken to me before. He said, "I was right here when you experienced the first ugly moment of your life. In fact, I have always been here. I comforted you through this man and modeled how I wanted you to live your life and bring comfort to those who need comforting. I have allowed all the tragic things in your life to occur knowing that you would be a vessel that I could use to bring healing to others. I was always with you, and you were never alone."

Can you imagine the revelation that was occurring in that moment? To have everything in your life suddenly make sense all at once? It's more magnificent than words can describe. God couldn't give me this revelation until I was ready to receive it. But because God is all-powerful and all-knowing, He knew when this moment was going to occur for me.

I have been blessed to minister to countless people over the years. God has used my personal experiences throughout my life to help others. Some of those experiences include divorce from a child's perspective, blended families both as a child and young adult, the cancer battle that my wife endured, the cancer battle that I endured, and the death of my son, to name a few. All of these circumstances can be made worse by the absence of the 12 most important words. There were many times when the 12 most important words would have been helpful for my own personal healing. So, God has used me to help people remove walls that separate them from their friends and loved ones, and to help prevent walls from forming in the future. I can only imagine that this is why He asked me to write this book. Imagine if everyone in the world spoke the 12 most important words to those they have harmed. Imagine if the 12 most important words were not simply spoken but were heartfelt and sincere (without wax) in delivery.

You might ask, "What does *'without wax'* mean?" The word sincere literally means "without hypocrisy!" The ancient Latins had a marketplace expression (sin cera) from which we derive our word sincere. When pottery makers wanted to advertise the quality of their wares, they labeled them sin cera, which meant "without wax." Dishonest potters were known to trick customers by filling the cracks in their pottery with wax to hide the flaws. When the pots were heated, both the cracks of the pottery and the hypocrisy of the potters were revealed. Real sincerity displays its cracks. The man who said to Jesus, "I believe; help my unbelief!" was exercising sincerity-without hypocritical wax.

> *Mark 9:24 (NIV), 'Immediately the boy's father exclaimed, "I do believe; help me overcome my unbelief!"'*

In spite of imperfections, it is the sincere person that catches the world's attention. Now imagine what our world might look like if each person shared the 12 most important words with real sincerity (no wax). With no wax we might begin to see the absence of walls. Can you imagine that?

-Not for one minute-

If we claim to love someone, why would we want them to feel like they are less than, offended, unloved, or rejected for even one minute? If any one of us were asked this question directly, I think it would be safe to say that we would all answer that question with a resounding, "No way! I would not want that to happen. I would not want my loved one to feel hurt or rejected." If my assumption is correct, how then do we explain the amount of hurt, pain, and conflict in our relationships? If we all desire that our loved ones would not be wounded either intentionally or unintentionally, then why do so many of our personal relationships have conflict and/or walls? The answer is simple. Every human being has good intentions but poor follow through. We would not want our loved ones to be upset or wounded, yet we hurt and wound them and then don't humble ourselves to be in a posture to do what it takes to make it right. Lip service at its finest. Why do we do this?

> *Romans 7:15-20 (NIV), "I do not understand what I do. For what I want to do I do not do, but what I hate I do. And if I do what I do not want to do, I agree that the law is good. As it is, it is no longer I myself who do it, but it is sin living in me. For I know that good itself does not dwell in me, that is, in my sinful nature. For I have the desire to do what is good, but I cannot carry it out. For I do not do the good I want to do, but the evil I do not want to do—this I keep on doing. Now if I do what I do not want to do, it is no longer I who do it, but it is sin living in me that does it."*

How do we prevent ourselves from repeating the same mistakes over and over? Our greatest asset is the time that we give. Our greatest gifts are the relationships that we foster. If we wound our loved ones over and over and don't learn to sincerely put the 12 most important words into practice, walls will eventually be erected to keep us out and we will be in danger of not being able to experience the development of our greatest gifts and time will slip away from us.

I know a man who in most every way is what the world would describe as good. He has many amazing qualities which include being a hard worker, strong, skilled, timely, likable, friendly, outgoing, polished, athletic, generous, kind, willing to lend a hand, trustworthy, stable, dependable, and an animal lover. However, like every other human, he also has unfavorable qualities that include being prideful, dishonest, narcissistic, selfish, careless, mean, unreliable, disloyal, untrustworthy, self-absorbed, inconsiderate, unable to take criticism, and places himself above others. Unfortunately, like many others, he is blind to his unfavorable qualities and how they inflict pain on those who love him. To make things worse, he appears to be lost when it comes to repairing his damaged relationships. Is it because he doesn't care or is there a deeper underlying reason for his inability to restore broken relationships due to his poor behavior?

Let's not forget that every person possesses these good and bad qualities. But make no mistake, each of us gets to choose when these less than favorable qualities are displayed. Sometimes they poke their heads out; even though we didn't mean for them to. That's exactly why the 12 most important words should always be on the tips of our tongues. In the case of the man that I was referring to, he has decided that the 12 most important words are not worth sharing with the people he hurts. It's not that he hasn't been approached about those unsavory characteristics, because I have personally approached him more times than I can count. In the 40 plus years that I have been approaching him, countless conversations have taken place regarding his need for a behavior change, but time after time I've been met with the same maddening reality of not seeing any change. Unfortunately for me and his loved ones, this is not an exaggeration. Keep in mind that when we approach a person about something they are doing wrong, our goal should never be to condemn them but always to see them restored.

Galatians 6:1 (NIV), "Brothers and sisters, if someone is caught in a sin, you who live by the Spirit should restore that person gently. But watch yourselves, or you also may be tempted."

This man had me believing for years that I was the person who was causing all of the hurt and turmoil in our relationship because he would always blame me for the things that went wrong. There were times when I thought I was crazy. But as time went on, more and more people were hurt by his incessant behavior and total lack of concern for others. I believe he now has at least 13 walls with his name on them that I know of. One of those walls he will never be able to break through. He won't be able to repair it because one of the people he wounded without ever sharing the 12 most important words, died way too young. God only knows if he will ever attempt to repair the others.

How can I know so many intimate details about this man's qualities, both positive and negative, and the walls that have been built, one brick of bad behavior after another, that were erected to keep him out of their lives? I know these details because the man I am referring to is my father. The walls with his name on them were built by my brothers, our wives, and our children. The wall that my father has no chance of repairing belongs to my son, Michael. As God would have it, there is always something of value to glean in every circumstance. My father taught my brothers and I what *not* to do, and for that I am grateful. One thing is for certain, not for one minute will I allow my loved ones to feel hurt and pain caused by me and my bad behavior. I pray for you always, Dad.

Jeff Frick

-iOS18-

Anyone who knows me knows that I am not a technical person. I get frustrated easily around any kind of technology, especially if it doesn't function the way that I'm used to. One time I was asked to take a selfie of the group I was with. When I placed the phone at the furthest distance I could reach to make sure everyone was in view, all I could see was the sky. "Where is everyone? I don't see us," I chuckled. It was then that a person from our group showed me that the camera had to be inverted in order to take the selfie. To most people, these so-called technical functions are not very technical at all. But for me, technology is my kryptonite. So, when my Apple iPhone prompted me to download iOS18 mid-way through the year, I downloaded it and followed the prompts. But when my iPhone returned to working mode after the download was complete, my phone was vastly different than it was prior to the update.

I sat in my chair trying to figure out all the changes that had been made to my phone. One area that bothered me more than the rest was my Photos app. It seemed to me that all my pictures were still there, but everything was changed in terms of format and placement. There were all kinds of new functions, menus, and options. I was growing more and more frustrated trying to figure out how to make sense of all that had changed. Then something caught my eye. I was staring at a new album that I had not created. The album was scrolling through the photos saved in my phone on its own. I watched the album play through the pictures twice before I finally realized what had happened.

The album was filled with pictures of me and my grandson, Jack. When I watched the album begin to scroll for the third time, I heard God say to me, "You have now spent more time with Jack in the 17 short months of his life, than either of your grandfathers spent with you in your entire life and more time than your father spent with your sons in their entire lives. A generational curse has been lifted and changed." At a moment when I was more than frustrated and in the least likely of ways, God demonstrated His goodness as only He can.

> *Ephesians 3:20-21 (NIV), "Now to him who is able to do immeasurably more than all we ask or imagine, according to his power that is at work within us, to him be glory in the church and in Christ Jesus throughout all generations, for ever and ever! Amen."*

What happens when we devote ourselves to the Lord? What happens when we live in such a way that brings glory and honor to Him? What I can tell you is this: He has so much He wants to reveal to us. We have no way of knowing what will happen in our lives; but one thing is for sure, He will honor those who honor Him. I encourage you to freely, intentionally and sincerely, use the 12 most important words when they are needed. When you humble yourself and use the 12 most important words, walls that are separating you from your loved ones will be removed. One day, when you least expect it, God will demonstrate something so marvelous that you couldn't possibly take the credit for it. He wants good things for us. He wants us to love others as He loves us. He doesn't want us to be separated from Him or from each other. To be close to Him and have the relationship with our loved ones that most of us crave, requires us to take action instead of being passive. Our part is not setting goals. Our part is to walk with Him and then reap the harvest that He has in store for each of us. You could never dream of the joyous blessings He has for you. Walls removed and generational curses lifted are just a few of the blessings He can provide. What blessings does He have waiting for you? I encourage you to walk with Him and find out.

> *Joel 1:2-3 (NIV), "Hear this, you elders; listen, all who live in the land. Has anything like this ever happened in your days or in the days of your ancestors? Tell it to your children, and let your children tell it to their children, and their children to the next generation."*

-No regrets-

In the progression of every person's life, there will be a "last time" to speak and spend time with every person that we love. Make no mistake, this will be the last time you will have to set things right, the last time to repair what is broken, the last time to say what you've always intended to say, and the last time to embrace. Were the 12 most important words needed because a relationship was distant, splintered, or fractured? Were you too busy waiting for the other person to do for you what you were unwilling to do for them? Were you holding the other person to a higher standard than the standard you placed on yourself? Did you share the 12 most important words or was it too late?

None of us know *when* these moments will occur, but we aren't ignorant to the fact that these moments *will* occur. Unfortunately, most of us are callous in our willingness to think ahead to these moments and are sometimes filled with regret over how things could have been instead of the reality of how they were when our loved one was here. When the inevitable happens to your loved one, will you have regrets over a dented and bruised relationship that you were waiting for them to begin to mend, instead of starting the mending process yourself? Were you not willing to scale the wall so that piece by piece, the bricks could be removed, and the healing begin?

Friends, I encourage you to evaluate your relationships with the people you love. Do you need to extend grace or perhaps ask for grace to be extended to you? Do you need to start a dialogue but don't have the words to begin? Have things gone so awry in the relationship that it feels as if it's almost not worth trying to salvage because it's littered with the metaphorical dents, bumps and bruises of hurled words from wanting to be heard, but not wanting to listen? If this is the reality you're facing, you have the choice of keeping the walls with your name on them and using them as a shield of deflection like my father *or* to let the photo album of your relationship scroll through your mind as a reminder of wanting to do things differently, like my realization with my grandson, Jack. If you want change, for things to be different, to be restored and renewed, start by humbling yourself and using the 12 most important words. It's not always easy and may take some time, but time spent in the relationship restoration process is *never* time wasted. Let me say that one more time. **Time spent in the relationship restoration process is never time wasted!**

> *James 3:18 (NIV),* "Peacemakers who sow in peace reap a harvest of righteousness."

A little more than five years ago, a "last time" occurred in my life. Like everyone else, I had no idea it would be my last time. How did it go? I have examined and thought about the last time I saw my son Michael, many, many times. I kept waiting for the regrets to surface. Did I have some? Of course. What were they? The regrets were of his sudden loss. The regrets were of lost opportunities long ago. The regrets were those that come with grief. I wrote down my thoughts as they formed:

The anticipation of April 11, 1997, brought joy, fear, and pain to my heart. Having already one son, would my heart be big enough for another? Yes! Yes, love abounds joyously! New mothers and fathers sometimes wonder how love can expand beyond their first child. The experience of their first child brings a love that cannot be

harnessed by words. So, when the second child is on the way, they sometimes sit in grief because they don't understand. They soon find out that love does abound.

We took having him in our lives for granted. Perhaps we all take having each other in our lives for granted as well?

I didn't know how much I loved him until he was gone.

When we gather now there's always someone missing.

"Michael, we never said goodbye."

What about the times he was wonderful, and I did nothing to acknowledge him, choosing to remain silent?

What about the times I was angry with him, or hurt him with my words?

What about the times I saw him sad and did little to nothing to console him?

What about the times I placed work ahead of being with him?

He was a gift to us for 22 years. Only when the gift was snatched away, did I truly realize how great it was. Then I could not tell him.

Pictures that once brought joy are now hard to look at.

"I miss you, Michael."

On July 7, 2019, the unrelenting pain of my broken heart, of death, and of "the no mores" began to outweigh the gratitude I once felt. Something is over. In the deepest levels of my existence something is finished. Done. Final. The pain of suffering is a guest to many. One day the guest became an owner. This gaping wound in my chest, — does it heal?

What before I did not see, I now see. What before I did not feel, I now feel. But this raw bleeding cavity which needs so much healing, does it heal? I want to ask for Michael back, but I can't. My tears have been my food for many days.

Jeff Frick

What is suffering? What it is, I do not know. I have reflected on it for too long. Still, I understand nothing of it. Of pain, yes! Suffering is a mystery, deep as any in our existence. Suffering keeps its face hidden from each while making itself known to all. Suffering is for the loving. If I hadn't loved him, there would not be this agony. Love suffers!

All of those regrets are tied to my loss, my grief, and my lost opportunities. However, the regret that I thankfully do not have to bear is for a broken relationship with my son. That is not to say that at one point our relationship was not in distress. But by the grace of God, I was moved to reconcile and build a relationship with Michael that was beautiful. Losing him will always be painful. My life would be nothing short of agony if I had done nothing to restore our relationship. But not having to hold onto a regret because our relationship was strong is both liberating and peaceful. My heavenly Father, His grace and mercy, and the 12 most important words are the sole reasons that I can walk in freedom today.

I implore you, digest the words that can change everything in your relationships. Eat them every day until they become a part of you. Share them freely with every person that you value and love. Intentionally sharing these words... *I was wrong. I am sorry. Please forgive me. I love you...* will help each of us live in relationships that flourish instead of being separated behind walls.

Now go, don't hesitate another moment, and share the words with others that have been given to you.

> *Ezekiel 3:1-5 (NIV), "And he said to me, "Son of man, eat what is before you, eat this scroll; then go and speak to the people of Israel." So I opened my mouth, and he gave me the scroll to eat. Then he said to me, "Son of man, eat this scroll I am giving you and fill your stomach with it." So I ate it, and it tasted as sweet as honey in my mouth. He then said to me: "Son of man, go now to the people of Israel and speak my words to them. You are not being sent to a people of obscure speech and strange language, but to the people of Israel—"*

Salvation Prayer

There's probably a good chance that not everyone who reads this book knows Jesus. For those who have yet to ask Jesus into your heart as Lord and Savior and receive the gift of salvation, please read this prayer, and be filled with the Holy Spirit. You may not know it yet, but soon enough you will realize that you belong to Jesus!

Lord Jesus, for too long I've kept You out of my life. I know that I am a sinner and that I cannot save myself. No longer will I close the door when I hear You knocking. By faith I gratefully receive Your gift of salvation. I am ready to trust You as my Lord and Savior. Thank You, Lord Jesus, for coming to earth. I believe You are the Son of God who died on the cross for my sins and rose from the dead on the third day. Thank You for bearing my sins and giving me the gift of eternal life. I believe Your words are true. Come into my heart, Lord Jesus, and be my Savior. Fill me with Your Holy Spirit. Amen.

Romans 10:9-10 (NIV), 'If you declare with your mouth, "Jesus is Lord," and believe in your heart that God raised him from the dead, you will be saved. For it is with your heart that you believe and are justified, and it is with your mouth that you profess your faith and are saved.'

Jeff Frick

Scripture References

Dedication
Numbers 6:24-26

Acknowledgments
1 Thessalonians 1:2

Author's Note
1 John 3:16
Philippians 4:4-9
Proverbs 18:21

1
Proverbs 28:13
Proverbs 24:16
Ecclesiastes 1:18
Matthew 19:4-6
Ephesians 4:2-3
Luke 15:20-24
Luke 15:3-7
Mark 10:6-9
Proverbs 31:10-11
Titus 1:6-7
Psalm 127:3
Proverbs 22:6
1 Peter 4:8
Luke 6:43-45
Romans 14:12
Proverbs 16:25
Galatians 5:22-25
Galatians 5:16-18
Proverbs 25:28
Proverbs 4:23

2

1 John 1:8
Philippians 2:5-11
Ecclesiastes 11:5
Ephesians 5:25-28
1 Corinthians 9:19-23
Isaiah 53:3-6
Deuteronomy 31:8
1 Peter 3:8
Isaiah 43:19
1 Corinthians 13:11

3

Just Say I'm Sorry, Source: Musixmatch; Songwriters: Alicia Moore / Christopher Alvin Stapleton; Just Say I'm Sorry lyrics © Pink Inside Publishing, I Wrote These Songs
Galatians 2:20
John 14:27
Isaiah 46:9-11
Proverbs 12:15
Luke 14:11
Proverbs 21:23
Ephesians 4:29
Proverbs 15:4
Ecclesiastes 4:9-12
1 John 4:19-21
Matthew 12:35-37
Proverbs 27:2
Ephesians 6:1-4
Jeremiah 29:11
Mattthew 6:14-15

4

Psalm 103:12
Luke 23:34
Matthew 18:21-22
2 Corinthians 1:3-5

Romans 12:1-2
1 Corinthians 9:27
Romans 12:3-8
Psalm 34:18
Galatians 6:7-8
Romans 13:8
Luke 2:52
Romans 16:19
Coat of Many Colors, Source: Musixmatch; Songwriters: Jonathon Smith/ Leeland Mooring/ Steven Furtick/ Andy Cherry/ Brandon Lake/ Jacob Boyles; Coat of Many Colors lyrics © Integrity's Praise Music, All Essential Music, Be Essential Songs, The Devil Is A Liar! Publishing
Hebrews 4:16
John 10:10
Psalm 147:3

5
1 John 3:18
John 3:16
Romans 5:6-8
1 John 4:16
Ephesians 4:22-24
1 John 4:7-8
James 1:19-20
Proverbs 12:18
Proverbs 17:17
Hebrews 6:10
1 Thessalonians 4:13-18
Ephesians 3:14-19
1 Thessalonians 2:8
Ecclesiastes 3:11
Psalm 37:3-4
Psalm 66:16-20
Philippians 1:3-4
Isaiah 45:3
James 4:13-15

Proverbs 3:3-4

6
Colossians 3:12-14
Psalm 1:1-3
2 John 1:9
Matthew 6:9-13
Romans 12:9-10
Hebrews 12:14
Dr. Loren Siffring, Loren's Musings (Self Published, 2016) Pg. 11
John 13:34-35
Romans 8:28
Psalm 139
Mark 9:24
Romans 7:15-20
Galatians 6:1
Ephesians 3:20-21
Joel 1:2-3
James 3:18
Ezekiel 3:1-5

Salvation Prayer
Romans 10:9-10

Other Books by Jeff

How do I Love my *Neighbor*? 4 PROMISES AND 6 TRUTHS
available on Amazon and Audible

IDENTITY MATTERS- The Power of BELONGING
available on Amazon and Audible

Jeff Frick

About The Author

Jeff is a pastor, chaplain, teacher, mentor, pastoral care provider, speaker, and author. He lives with his wife Laura in Shelby Township, Michigan, and they have been married for more than 33 years. He is a father, a grandfather, a brother, an uncle, a son, and a friend to many. He has served in various organizations over the years in the community in which he lives. Jeff is involved in discipling men in several churches in the local Detroit area.

Jeff's passions include reading, writing, teaching, mentoring, counseling, and discipling men. He is a life-long learner and shares his knowledge with the dozens he counsels and serves. He is also founder/president of GRAM (**G**od **R**efines **A**ll **M**en, **G**od **R**edeems **A**ll **M**en, **G**od **R**estores **A**ll **M**en) Ministry. His ministry, of more than two decades, has primarily been in small groups and one-on-one encounters.

Many long-established spiritual leaders have poured into Jeff over the years. He believes this spiritual capital God has poured into him should be invested into the lives of others. Jeff spends his days encouraging men to receive the grace of our Father in Heaven and to trust Jesus, His Son, as their life Source and purpose.

Jeff Frick

www.ingramcontent.com/pod-product-compliance
Lightning Source LLC
Chambersburg PA
CBHW030939090426
42737CB00007B/482